# Illalong Children

## A. B. (Banjo) Paterson

# Illalong Children

## A. B. (Banjo) Paterson

illustrated by Robert Lovett

Lansdowne
Sydney • Auckland • London • New York

Published by Lansdowne, Sydney
a division of RPLA Pty Limited
176 South Creek Road, Dee Why West, N.S.W., Australia, 2099
First published in this format 1985
Text: Copyright Reserved
© Retusa Pty Limited 1983
Illustrations: Copyright Reserved
© Retusa Pty Limited 1985
Produced in Australia by the Publisher
Typeset in Australia by Savage Type Pty Ltd, Brisbane
Printed in Hong Kong by Dai Nippon Printing Co. (H.K.) Ltd

**National Library of Australia Cataloguing-in-Publication Data**

Paterson, A. B. (Andrew Barton), 1864–1941.
Illalong children.

ISBN 0 7018 1805 0.

1. Paterson, A. B. (Andrew Barton), 1864–1941.
2. Poets, Australian — Biography. I. Lovett,
Robert. II. Title.

A821′ .2

# Contents

# Introduction

THIS ALL began with the questions of a little four-year-old girl, with all her life before her: and the questions were asked of me, a grandfather with all his life behind him.

'Tell me about when you were a little boy,' she said, 'when you lived in the bush. What was it like? Did you always have damper for breakfast? Did you wear riding breeches and a red shirt like the man in the pictures? How many dogs had you, and how many horses?'

So that started it. Seventy years of it, and I had to think of something that would interest a child.

But perhaps it will be better to clear the ground first, and come to the experiences later on.

This is the story of a bush family, living firstly in the western and later the southern district of New South Wales. The date was 1874 and a few years on either side of that. Apart from two infants, the family consisted of my father and mother, my two elder sisters Jessie and Flo, my cousin Jack Paterson, who lived with us after his father died, and, of course, myself. We four children could read and write but our time was usually occupied in other pursuits. My story is told with the view of giving my grandchildren some idea of the life of children on a country station in those far-off days.

# First Impressions

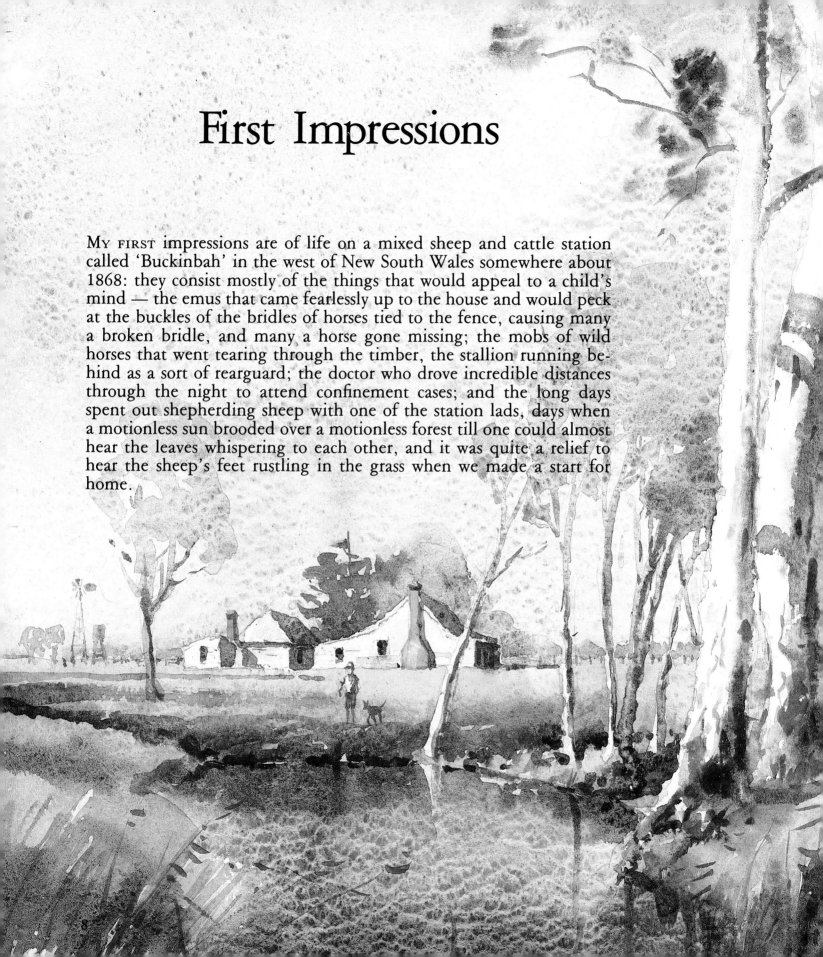

My FIRST impressions are of life on a mixed sheep and cattle station called 'Buckinbah' in the west of New South Wales somewhere about 1868: they consist mostly of the things that would appeal to a child's mind — the emus that came fearlessly up to the house and would peck at the buckles of the bridles of horses tied to the fence, causing many a broken bridle, and many a horse gone missing; the mobs of wild horses that went tearing through the timber, the stallion running behind as a sort of rearguard; the doctor who drove incredible distances through the night to attend confinement cases; and the long days spent out shepherding sheep with one of the station lads, days when a motionless sun brooded over a motionless forest till one could almost hear the leaves whispering to each other, and it was quite a relief to hear the sheep's feet rustling in the grass when we made a start for home.

My father was away from home a lot, looking after our Queensland place, and my mother was busy from daylight till dark with household work. The result was that I spent most of my time down at the men's hut. Here there lived old Jerry and his son, whose surnames I never knew, but they were fascinating company. Jerry was a shepherd, tall, bearded and straight as a sapling with a rugged face and deeply sunken eyes. He told me that there were plenty of fairies in the country where he came from, but you could never recognise them 'unless you happened to sneak up on one of them while he was washing his face so as you could see what he was like'. To the station hands he was known as 'Jerry the Rhymer', as sometimes in his talk he would start off using rhyming words without seeming to know that he did it. For instance, discussing his son's dogs, his tongue would seem to run away with him and he would say, 'Baldie and Nigger gets bigger and bigger, with eating their muttons like so many gluttons, and if we don't stop 'em, your Pa'll have to whop 'em'. Poor enough stuff, but it sounded wonderful to a small boy, especially from a man who could neither read nor write.

Years afterwards down Yass way I met another of these rhymers, and in his case, too, it seemed that he *had* to rhyme, rather than that he wished to rhyme. Old Jerry was something of a celebrity in the district, as it was rumoured that he had left the old country for some minor offence which he had never committed, but he had done very much worse things which had never been found out: so that he was ahead of the authorities on points by a clear margin. A queer life, his, out all day with his sheep, seeing nobody, unable to read, alone with his memories. He might have taken to wearing corks round his hat, which was generally regarded as a prelude to a mental examination, only that he had been a fo'c'sle hand in the days of sail and he had all sorts of ways of occupying himself.

He could plait greenhide stockwhips with carved myall wood handles and he would spend hours thinking out the proper weight and length of the 'fall'. He did the killing for the station, and, with an oilstone, he kept his knives like razors. Nor would any oilstone or any knife do him. He was a virtuoso in oilstones and knives; and, when a travelling hawker tried to sell him an oilstone and a knife, he said that the stone would blunt the best knife that ever was forged and, as for the knife, he said it was no use to him as he hadn't seen butter for months.

He was a great hand on bees' nests and, if he happened to find one in a tree near the homestead, he would let me go out with him and sit on a log at a safe distance while he felled the tree with an axe which could have been used for shaving. Then he would light a small fire with plenty of smoke at the entrance to the nest and so bewilder the bees that they hardly put up any fight at all. Once, the fall of the tree cracked the bees' nest wide open and, when he went up to make his fire, the bees came at him in battalions, paying particular attention to the back of his neck. Sitting on my log, I was horrified to see my hero legging it through the bush like a two-year-old, beating himself with his hands and finally jumping in the only dam within fifty miles. 'Scat them bees,' he said. ' 'Tis lucky I was a great runner wanst. If I hadn't bet [beaten] their main swarm to the dam, I was a dead man.'

Then there was the straining of the honey in the little open-faced bark shed at the back of his hut, a ceremony attended by all the bees in the district. It was strained through a sugar bag — a sugar bag so open in its construction that it let the bees' legs and wings and little grains of box dust come through, along with the honey. By the time the straining was finished some of the visiting bees had drowned themselves in the honey and had to be fished out. The resultant mixture, what with a *soupcon* of bees' legs and a fine flavouring of yellow box timber, was something that a man could get his teeth into. He always had a hot damper ready by the time the honey was strained, and after I had been sent up to the homestead to borrow some butter he would cut great slices of yellow damper and spread half an inch of butter and half an inch of honey on each slice. 'There's people,' he said, 'would think I was putting too much butther and honey on the damper, but 'tis such a fine damper, ye wouldn't taste the butther and honey without I put on plenty.' He had no use at all for the bread baked up at the house from home-made yeast brewed by my mother and the girl in the kitchen. 'Makin' a sort of sour paste out of hops,' he said, 'and callin' it yeast. Now, if yer Ma will give me them hops I'll brew some honey beer would make a native bear dance a jig.'

Some philosopher has said, 'Blessed is the man who has found his work', and I found my first job of work at the age of about four. A police trooper arrived at the homestead one night, having ridden fifty miles to get a warrant from my father for the arrest of one of our own shepherds. No other Justice of the Peace was available, nor was my father available, as he had just left for Queensland. A traveller had been held up on the road and was robbed of a lot of gold, and the usual informer had come along and told the police that our shepherd had received the gold from the robber and was hiding it in his hut until the skies cleared a bit. The policeman had to go back home and look for another J.P., and my mother did not know what she should do or whether she should do anything in the affair, as Howard (the suspect shepherd) had always seemed decent enough. Recourse was had to old Jerry, who said that Howard had as many names as the King of England and knew his way round.

'He'll clear out,' he said. 'He'll get the word from the township. I'll bet he's got it now. There'd be a man on the road with it the minnit the bobby left the township. See here, now. Send my son, young Jimmy, out to bring in Howard's sheep and Jimmy can shepherd 'em from here until you get somebody else. You can't leave the sheep starven in the yard.' Sound advice, too, for when young Jimmy got out there, Howard had departed and the sheep were wondering when somebody would come along and let them out.

Jimmy was appointed deputy shepherd, vice Howard, with orders to work close to the homestead, and I suppose I must have been a bit of a nuisance about the place, for I was told that I could go out with young Jimmy every day and learn to be a shepherd. Nobody who has anything to do with sheep ever forgets it, but that must keep for another chapter.

# Shepherding

IN THE last chapter, something was said about life on a western station and the events which led up to my going out shepherding a mob of sheep with one of the station boys.

But first as to the scenery and surroundings. Our house stood on an open plain with a creek at the back which sometimes came down a banker and sometimes had next to no water in it. This creek provided us with one of our few games. A friend of the family, one 'Billy' Forster, had been cast away with his companions from a small schooner somewhere up on the Barrier Reef, and was supposed to be living with the wild blacks or, perhaps, the blacks were living on him. A rescue party, including my uncle, Edward Barton, had gone up in the brig *Maria* to see what could be done about it, and every time that a flood came down bringing logs and snakes and sundries with it, my young sister and I would sit on the bank of the creek, fascinated by the roar of water. If a log came past with a snake on it we called that log the brig *Maria*; and if it got past us and out of sight without being rolled over or sucked under, we reckoned that the brig *Maria* would return in safety from her voyage with the rescued men aboard. It worked, too, for the castaways came back without loss of life.

Away up in front of the house, the (unfenced) country stretched for miles and miles. Flat country, with big belts of timber and patches of scrub. Here it was that we had to do our shepherding — old Jerry's son Jim, aged about twelve, his two dogs Baldie and Nigger and my juvenile self. Young Jim left nothing to be desired in my eyes, for he could ride, could boil a billy and could track the sheep if ever we let them stray out of sight in the timber. But even at the age of twelve he had his troubles. The dingoes were bad and might rush the sheep at any moment and his father, old Jerry, had promised him a hiding if he let the two mobs get boxed. It was my first experience of responsibility, and I spent the first few days with one eye out for dingoes and the other out for Jerry's sheep. Nothing happened and, as children will, we forgot our worries and settled down to enjoy ourselves. Every morning we let the mob out of their yard built of saplings stood on end as high as a man and laced together with wire to keep out the dingoes. Leaving the yard, we would let the sheep draw off across the plain where there was every chance of a kangaroo rat springing out from its grass-lined nest right under our feet and setting off across the plain with the two dogs after it. These coursing matches always ended one way, in victory for the kangaroo rat, but we always had some excuse for the dogs. Either they had eaten too much or too little, or the ground was too hard or too soft — anything rather than admit that the kangaroo rat was too good. It was something the same with the emus, which the dogs pursued very half-heartedly. As young Jimmy explained it, 'If ever the dogs caught up to 'em, one of them things could turn round and kick a dog's head off, just as easy as you'd knock the head off a thistle.' One day we walked right on to a hen emu with a brood of chickens, just after we got the sheep in among the timber. The sight of the chickens started the dogs off in great style; but the old hen emu stuck her head out like a snake and made for the dogs with her feathers rustling and her great hard feet pounding the ground. The next hundred yards or so provided a fine chase, with the two dogs just a length in front and doing their best for once in a way.

Sometimes young Jimmy would cut throwing sticks with his tomahawk and would try to knock a native bear out of a tree. When struck, they would cry like children, and this upset me greatly until Jimmy explained that it was all for their own good. 'A bear'll sit in a fork till he takes root,' he said, 'without somebody'll tap him wit' a stick and make him climb up higher. An' you can't hurt 'em; bears is stronger than bullicks. If they was as big as bullicks, then two bears could pull a waggon of wool. The only thing stronger'n a bear is a wombat. I seen three big dogs onto a wombat one day an' he walked off to his burrow with 'em and them diggin' their feet into the ground.'

Then came the black day, the day when the two mobs got boxed. I never knew whose fault it was, but I knew that Jimmy would get the blame. Sheep are the champion passive resisters of the world, and the only time that they take any interest in anything is when they see another mob of sheep. Our mob was on the edge of one belt of timber and old Jerry's mob was on the edge of another belt about half a mile away. With the determination to do the wrong thing which distinguishes sheep above all other of the animal kingdom, the two mobs made for each other, baa-ing loudly.

I do not know what old Jerry was doing, but Jimmy at the time was up a sapling after a wild silkworm's nest. He slid down the sapling, tearing his hands and clothes, and sent Baldie and Nigger at top speed in between the two flocks. Not a hope. A hundred dogs wouldn't have stopped them.

My own idea is that old Jerry had been asleep under a tree, for he never showed up until the mobs were so mixed that separating them would have been like unscrambling scrambled eggs. Not a word was heard as we marched the two mobs back to the homestead. It meant a day's work drafting them and a day's hunger and knocking about for the sheep. The sheep put up with it with their usual lack of interest in life. I suppose they thought the sorrow was divided about fifty-fifty between them and their owners, and when a sheep comes out anywhere near square with anybody, he thinks he is doing rather well. They don't expect much.

Jimmy expected his beating and his father duly kept his word. They had their own sense of dignity, these 'old hands', the dignity of men who had suffered. They had been disciplined in their day and they felt that it was only right that their sons should know discipline. Not like the sons of the free settlers who were brought up anyhow, like young wild horses. I knew several of these old hands in the early days and, whatever their failings might have been, they always kept order in their families. A swagman who came along with a dog was engaged as shepherd and that closed the incident.

I was sorry to give up shepherding, as my sister and I had no play-mates, never saw any other children, and such strangers as came along were just as likely to be bad characters, dodging the police. I remember my mother loading a gun (muzzle-loader) in the sitting-room one evening when all the men were away and a particularly villainous-looking stranger had cast up. Putting the hammer down, she let it slip and the gun went off with a frightful bang, bringing down a shower of whitewash from the calico ceiling and scaring the life out of a family of possums who lived up among the beams and were just preparing to go out for the night. I suppose the stranger must have heard the shot down in the travellers' hut, for he was very civil when he came along in the morning to draw his meat, tea and sugar: 'And if you could spare a bit of bread, lady, I'd be glad of it. I ain't much hand at makin' damper.'

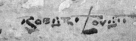

Shortly afterwards we moved to another station and that closed my career in the flat country, a country supposed to be dull and monotonous, but it had a charm of its own. Out in that dry air there is sometimes, just at daybreak, a false dawn when the eastern sky glows with all the colours of an opal. As the opal fades away it is succeeded by a pale silver sky, luminous as first-class pearl, and this in turn gives way before the rays of the rising sun. In that flat country we could see for illimitable distances, and the openings through the trees with the silver sky at the back looked like white-walled houses hiding among the timber. I could never get over the idea that there was a town there somewhere, if we could only find it. In the foreground the silver of the myall trees contrasted with the almost black frondage of the belah, the bronze of young leaves on the apple trees and the stiff, toylike pines which always reminded me of the trees in a Noah's Ark. Across the landscape moved mobs of kangaroos and flocks of emus, quaint uncanny creatures moving silently through that grey light like the creatures of a dream. If ever a great Australian play is written, the scene will be cast, not in the hills which never change, but in the flat country which can stage anything from the desolation of a drought to a sea of waving grasses, with a march of strange animals and a dance of queer, self-conscious birds.

# Arrival at 'Illalong'

WHEN I was seven years old, my Uncle John died and my father took charge at 'Illalong', the family's mountain station near Yass. Most parts of Australia are flat and dry, but this was hilly and wet. Some of the hills were very steep and rough with big patches of scrub where the kangaroos lay about in the shade during the heat of the day, just like shearers having a smoke during a spell. They threw themselves down on the ground in unstudied attitudes or they squatted on their haunches just as a shearer will sit on his heels, and some muscular shearers only need tails to be very like kangaroos, or, if a kangaroo had no tail, he would make a very passable shearer.

The young kangaroos, leaving their mothers' pouches, ran little races against each other over the rocks, round the big dead tree and back again, causing their mothers some worry lest they should bruise the pads of their hind feet on the rocks or jump across the wombat holes instead of going round them.

A wombat hole looks as though some unskilful person had sunk a shaft for gold, and is generally masked by long grass so that it is just the sort of place which might give anyone a very nasty fall. Not that this would worry the wombat, for he has his suite of rooms right away down at the bottom of his burrow and he never worries about anything. He avoids all thought so carefully that if he wants to move out of his bedroom into his sitting-room, he just stops where he is: it saves trouble.

In some parts of these hills, too, there were sheer cliff walls where a fall meant a very bad smash indeed, but the little kangaroos kept away from these dangerous places. These cliffs were the home of the rock wallabies, queerly marked little fellows scarcely bigger than squirrels, with long, furry tails and with patches of colour over their eyes. They had no fear of the cliffs; in fact, they loved nothing so well as to start at the foot of a cliff and go up it, just touching a knob of rock here or getting a foothold in a tiny crack there, till they came to the top. The other animals were envious of these displays and thought that the rock wallabies were very flash people. Flasher still were the lyrebirds which spread their tails and pranced up and down on an open patch of rock, mimicking and making fun of every creature in the

17

bush. If the lyrebirds heard a new sound such as the crash of a splitter's axe or the tinkle of a bullock bell, they would practise it until they got it right; but they did not need to practise such sounds as the alarm cry of young parrots in a nest, causing the parrot mothers to hurry home to see what had gone wrong. What with one thing and another, the lyrebirds gave their neighbours a lot of trouble.

The 'Illalong' homestead was an old-fashioned cottage, built of slabs covered with plaster, whitewashed till it shone in the sun. The roof had originally been bark and when the bark got old and friable the bullock driver and Kerry the black boy would be sent out with axes to strip some more. They stripped it by cutting a seam down the side of a tree and then they wedged and hammered the bark until it became loose and at last it peeled off in a cylinder. They flattened this out and put logs on it so that it could not curl up again, and after a few days, when it had dried nice and flat, they went out with the bullock dray and brought in the load. Then they pulled the old bark off and stuck the new bark in place and, lo, they had a new roof. Then came the day when the dray arrived with a load of galvanised iron to make a permanent roof and this was put on over the bark for the sake of coolness. When it was first erected, the wild ducks, flying through the moonlight, would sometimes mistake the shining roof for a sheet of water and would land on it, thump, thump, thump, waking everybody out of their sleep and terrifying the ducks, who were quite ashamed of themselves for having made such a mistake. They soon learned the difference between a sheet of iron and a sheet of water and the roof gave every satisfaction, except that the possums would scamper backwards and forwards along the ridgepole and sometimes one of them would miss his footing and would slide down to the water-spouting, with his claws making the most frightful scratching sound. When one of them did this, the others would all chatter at him in their queer lingo, making fun of him, and the possum who had slid down would sit on the spouting at the edge of the verandah with his tail hanging over and would explain that this sort of roof was no good, a man couldn't get his claws into it. If anybody pulled his tail he would start straight up the roof again and would slip back, making more noise than ever.

The homestead ceilings were made of calico, whereon the possums used to run races in the evenings before going out into the garden for a feed. The children took a hand by trying to stick sharp instruments into the feet of the possums as they raced across the ceiling. On leaving the house, the possums used to jump from the roof onto a paling fence and run along it till they could leap into the foliage of a big elderberry tree. Armed with sticks, we youngsters used to wait under the shelter of the verandah and try to knock the possums off as they ran past. Brother Possum, however, has a keen eye at night and would only make his rush when his enemies had their minds distracted. They were quaint little fellows, the possums, with their inquisitive faces and their friendly ways. Gum leaves were their natural food, which gave them a fine aromatic eucalyptus smell; but they preferred fruit when they could get it, and small blame to them, for gum leaves must become very monotonous.

Among the night noises were the call of a mopoke, the whine of a native cat, or the bloodcurdling hooting of a powerful owl. The first time that one of these birds really let his voice go in the garden my father happened to be away, and nobody in the place could guess the source of these dreadful sounds. The girl in the kitchen, bush-reared, came in and explained matters. 'Don't you know what that is?' she said. 'It's a howl.' We were just going to ask her what was howling, when a great grey bird on noiseless wings drifted across the yard just over our heads and the banshee myth that might have been was exploded. At that, a powerful owl can give any banshee that ever lived a start and beat it at its own speciality.

Jack and I were just learning to ride on quiet station ponies, and we had, like our Scottish forebears, to contend with raiders. Not armed raiders, be it understood, but every year in the spring there flowed past the station a tide of shearers making out to the western sheds. Mostly they were mounted, but some were on foot, and these footsloggers had a habit of helping themselves to any quiet horse which they could catch in the paddock at night. These they would turn loose when they reached their destination and it was a matter of luck and police efficiency if they were ever recovered.

Horses were cheap enough, two pounds was about the average price for a good station pony; but it would have been a heartbreaking business if our mounts had disappeared. We took counsel from 'Old Harry', not the mythical personage of that name, but as stout a retainer as ever served a Scotsman. Old Harry was an English agricultural labourer who had been 'sent out' for poaching pheasants, and was a match for any raider. He was a 'Zummerzet' man. 'Pit yeer pownies in garden every night,' he said, 'and t'dorgs'll let ye know if owt comes after 'em.' Not only did we retain our ponies, but at the ages of about six and seven respectively we bought a horse for ourselves.

A man who described himself as 'an overlander who had just delivered some cattle' came into the station one day, leading a horse so poor and weak that it could hardly stagger along. The overlander, whose motto appeared to be 'Keep going', said that he would sell the horse if anyone would give him five shillings to cover his fare to Yass in the coach.

Everyone in authority was away, but there had been rain at the station and the old sheep yard at the back of the stables was covered with shoots of beautiful soft young herbage. We somehow raked up five shillings between us, and with the assistance of Old Harry, who knew nothing about horses, actually propped the animal up with a pole and fed it with handfuls of herbage. After it had eaten a good feed, we very reluctantly let it lie down.

Some hour or two later, we decided to get it up again, but Old Harry had gone away and we were unable to lift it. Then it suddenly struck us that the horse could eat just as well while lying on the ground; in fact, it seemed to prefer it, and for the rest of that day and the next we were carrying food to the patient. When my father came home, the horse could get up by himself, and could even walk about in a staggering sort of way.

'I don't mind your buying him,' said father, 'but I think your overlander must have found a horse which nobody had lost. I know his brand. He is a Queensland horse and I suppose the overlander was about a hundred miles ahead of the police. That horse might have belonged to some little boy like yourselves, and you wouldn't like a little Queensland boy to keep your ponies if anyone took them away. I'll have to write to the owner.' Two very gloomy boys waited till an answer came to that letter.

'The boys can keep the horse,' it said, 'but we would like to get hold of the man who pinched him. We have hundreds of horses up here, too many. If the boys are in the horse buying business, we can let them have as many as they want at five bob a head. We used to call that horse White-when-he's-wanted because the black boy who broke him in said, "By cripes, boss, this fella white when he's wanted." Tell the boys to go down to his fetlocks as if they were going to take hobbles off him when they want to catch him. All our horses are broken in that way, and when he freshens up he might give them a lot of trouble if they tried to catch him any other way. Good luck.'

When he recovered his health and strength, the Queenslander soon showed that he was no small boy's horse. He threw a visiting jackaroo and tried to strike him with his front feet while on the ground, a manoeuvre which the jackaroo foiled by rolling under a log. Then the horse was tried in harness, on the theory that he must have been created for some useful purpose. To everyone's amazement he went away as quietly as possible, nor did he ever misbehave himself except on the occasion when the blacksmith's boy in Yass unfortunately selected him, in place of his yoke-mate, for a ride up the street. He went out for a short ride and he got it. 'If I had known he was broke in by a black boy,' he said, 'I'd have blackened myself before I got on him.'

That episode was closed by the sale of the horse (guaranteed quiet to harness only) for five pounds, a very nice profit on five shillings.

# King Billy and his Family

IT WAS always a sorrow to the children that there was only one family of blacks in the district, but it consoled us a lot that the head of the tribe wore a brass plate round his neck inscribed, 'Billy Budgeree, King of the Lachlan'. It gave us a thrill to think that we were meeting royalty face to face, begging cold mutton for him from the cook, and hinting to father (who in our eyes was the usurper of Billy's throne) that he might spare a fig of tobacco from the store for Billy's insatiable pipe.

Mutton, tobacco, and (if he could get it) grog were the things always uppermost in Billy's mind. The girls thought that Billy's wife Sally should also wear a brass plate inscribed with her name and rank, 'Queen Sally of the Lachlan', but Sally had no ambition. Her comment was brief and pointed. 'What for you talk it longa old brassa plate? That fella no good. You got him tabac?'

Sally did not smoke as much tobacco as Billy, for one reason only — that she could not get as much. Their one child was a little girl, Nora by name, about six years of age and very stolid and silent among white children. They had been given these names by a bush missionary who happened to be a Baptist and believed in total immersion. Nora described the christening ceremony by saying, 'Close up that fella drown himself.' Nora could swim like a duck, and when the children asked Queen Sally how she had taught Nora to swim, she said, 'No more me bin teach 'um, me throw 'um in longa creek.'

The royal palace of King Billy was built of three saplings stuck in the ground and tied together at the top, while the walls were mouldering sheets of bark blown off the hay shed. A tattered old possum rug, a flour bag and a Government blanket seemed to be their only bedding; on cold nights their three dogs would crawl in with them and lend them the warmth of their bodies. A fire was always kept going in front of the humpy; a blackfellow's fire which never got any bigger or smaller, but was fed with just enough material to keep it going.

Queen Sally and her daughter wore calico dresses, but on cold days the Queen reinforced her wardrobe with the Government blanket, worn shawlwise over the shoulders. This, as she explained, was not only a protection against cold but also a precaution against theft. 'S'posin' me bin wear him, no feller bin steal him,' she said. The little black princess wore the flour bag for the same reasons and in the same way. The other portable property of the ladies of the Royal house was a 'dilly bag' made of twisted grass, and in this they carried anything from the remains of their last meal to a clutch of wild duck eggs. The royal arms of the King consisted of a tomahawk, a throwing spear propelled by a womerah and a white piece of stone. The tomahawk was used to shape boomerangs out of angular bits of timber; the throwing spear was more or less a superfluity, but was useful on occasions when the King was invited to give an exhibition of spear throwing. These invitations he always accepted with the proviso, 'You gib it nobbler.' No nobbler, no exhibition! The laws against supplying blacks with liquor were less stringently enforced than they are nowadays.

The remaining item, the piece of limestone, was stated by its owner to have the power of bringing rain anywhere at any time. In one drought when the sheep were dying, King Billy was asked to 'trot out his rainstone'. With a quick look at the sky he said, 'No more want him rain yet. Plenty feller grass. By em by, make it rain.'

The next day he said that there was 'plenty water longa creek', and then changed the subject; on the third day there were a few clouds about and he said, 'Debbil Debbil sit down; me go speak along Debbil Debbil.' Whatever the result of this conference with the powers of evil may have been, the fourth day was ushered in by a heavy roll-up of clouds and Billy proceeded with all the dignity of a Roman soothsayer to carry his rainstone down to the creek. Arrived at the creek, he placed the rainstone in a carefully selected spot, looked to the east, the west, the north and the south, and then pronounced the following incantation:

Rain come tumble down
Wheelbarrow broke it,
Old Mr Paterson
Wouldn't give us blanket.

The last two lines were by way of conveying a hint in a delicate manner.

Rain! It rained three inches that night. The creek came down a banker, and in the morning the frogs started to croak, the birds to sing, the wild duck and wild turkeys came in from all surrounding districts and the water rats displayed their black and gold coats in the exuberance of spring fashions. Not only had the station got rain, but the downfall seemed to have missed all other places.

Marching up to the boss, King Billy said, 'No got him tobacco, no got him sugar bag, what about it nobbler?' This was enough to take anyone's breath away.

My father said, 'S'pose I gibbit nobbler, you beat 'um gin, you beat 'um piccaninny, policeman kill you dead fellow. Me gibbit you three figs tobacco, plenty flour, plenty sugar, plenty tea. What happen that other Government blanket you got from policeman?'

'Me bin loss him,' whined Sally.

'You been let puppy dog tear him up, mine thinkit. Missis go look out old feller blanket for you.'

Thus was an honourable peace concluded, and King Billy's fame spread far and wide. Truth to tell, Billy had been looked upon as a cadging old nuisance at the neighbouring stations, and his dogs were in even less favour than himself. Now, he was told that he could come along and bring his dogs any time that he liked. They could not afford to overlook a rainmaker of his class.

# Spear Throwing

AFTER HIS success in rainmaking, King Billy was very little inclined to put himself out for anybody. In less than two days, he had dissipated all the rewards of that exploit. He had given away or smoked or eaten all the sugar, all the flour, all the tobacco and all the mutton. Nothing remained but an idea that his services had not been properly rewarded.

Thus it was that when we children asked him to give an exhibition of spear throwing, he refused point blank to do anything of the sort. In his mind, spear throwing and a nobbler followed each other as certainly as the night follows the day. He tossed his spear and womerah to Sally, saying, 'You throw him spear,' and stalked off.

Old Sally's skinny arms did not promise very much in the way of feats of strength, but willingness she had in plenty, for such a chance as this seldom came her way.

The womerah is a piece of stick about two feet long with a notch or crook at one end. Into this notch, the butt of the spear is fitted. Spear and womerah are then grasped in the right hand, and the leverage imparted by the womerah will make a spear go a surprising distance. Without a womerah it is difficult to throw a spear by hand more than a few yards; when thrown from a womerah, a spear becomes a dangerous weapon up to fifty yards.

Standing, as it were, under the spotlight of public observation, Sally posed her body in a position suggestive of Ajax defying the lightning, took aim at the butt of a tree and launched the spear. Straight to the mark it travelled, and stuck, quivering, in the bark. The dogs, which had watched with the utmost interest, at once took to flight, the station dogs making for shelter under the beds, while the blackfellows' dogs made a beeline for their camp, a route which involved swimming across the flooded creek. Among them was a small puppy, the delight of Sally's heart, and when Sally saw her beloved pup being swept down the creek among floating logs, sheep hurdles and boughs of dead trees, she dropped the womerah and ran to the rescue. It looked as though the spear throwing had come to a sudden end, but the youthful Nora saved the show. She stepped into the breach for the credit of the black race. Without saying a word, she trotted up to the tree, drew out the spear from the bark and placed herself exactly where her mother had

stood, adopting the same pose as her mother, and handling the spear and womerah like a professional. We could hardly believe that she could handle a spear at all; and, wishing to see better, I ran across the line of flight just as she let the spear go on its journey. Her throw was in no way comparable to that of her mother, for the spear began to drop when it had travelled ten yards; and it was just too bad that it landed fair on the calf of my leg. Aided no doubt by the momentum of its fall, it stuck about a quarter of an inch into the flesh. With the spear still trailing from my leg, I ran crying to my mother and the show broke up in confusion.

What a tragedy! A small boy speared in the calf of the leg by a black, and the spear still in the wound! But, after all, it was not so terrible. Similar accidents happened every day in the lives of station people, accidents such as falls from horses, accidents with axes, rescues of the apparently drowned. No one ever thought of sending twenty miles for a doctor, for were there not Farmer's Friend as a disinfectant, and Holloway's ointment to heal the wound? Did they not sing almost every evening on the woodheap the ballad which ran:

> All ye who long have pain endured
> Can rest content and be assured
> That every ailment can be cured
> By Holloway's pills and ointment?

The affair was not reported in any local newspapers, for there were no local papers; and the only ripple that it made on the slumbering pool of bush life was when one of the neighbouring station hands said to another, 'I hear that one of them kids at "Illalong" got a spear stuck in his leg by a black girl.' The other replied, 'Serve them right. Why did they let a woman throw a spear when there was kids about? She might have hit a horse.'

King Billy and his family soon afterwards disappeared from 'Illalong' in the purposeless, mysterious way common to blacks. Without warning or farewell they went on a 'walkabout', a sort of wanderlust which seizes all blacks at times. No matter how comfortable their circumstances, no matter whether they are in permanent employment, when the time comes it is a case of, 'My heart is turned to Dixie and I must go'. They can no more resist the call than the birds can resist the call to migration.

Let us hope that, in their new surroundings, King Billy's talents as a rainmaker were properly appreciated and that Sally and the diminutive Nora had 'plenty feller tucker'. They deserved it.

But if there were no more blacks in the experiences of the family, were there any bushrangers? One looks for bushrangers and blacks in any chronicle of early days in Australia, and it was owing to our experiences with the blacks that Jack and I got an inkling of what a 'sticking up' meant. We were invited to stay in the house of a gentleman who had, in defence of his wife and family, shot a bushranger. It was at Cunningham Plains station, near Murramburrah, twenty miles from 'Illalong', that we went to stay with Mr David Campbell, famous in the district as the man who shot O'Maley at Goimbla. He had later on removed to Cunningham Plains and at the time of our visit he was living there with his second wife and three sons of his first marriage; neighbours were few and far between, so we were brought along to play with the little Campbells.

Mr Campbell was no two-gun man of the Wild West type. Shy, quiet-spoken, and courteous, he left it to others to tell the story of the shooting, but an old station hand was still with him and had seen the whole thing.

'O'Maley and his mates,' he said, 'they had it in for the boss, I don't know why. Must have been somethin' he said about them and they got to hear of it. Anyhow, they come along to stick up Goimbla. It was just getting dark when they came. They must have reckoned they'd rob the place and get away without bein' reckonised. Mr and Mrs Campbell were in the house and the three kids were out in their room a few yards away from the house. The girls and I, we were in the kitchen at the back. You know in them days we were always on the lookout for bushrangers, and when we heard a rifle go off and the smack of a bullet agin a wall I says to the girl, ''Here they are.'' No, I didn't go out. I reckoned that bullet sounded as if it was in a hurry. They thought the boss would come out and surrender when he heard that bullet, but he's a game man, the boss. He ran for his rifle and fired at the place the sound came from. And, if he was game, what

about Mrs Campbell? She thought the youngsters would be frightened and she ran down to their room, and the bushrangers fired at her as she ran down. They were miserable murderin' hounds all right, shootin' at a woman. Then the boss sees, agin the skyline, a man's head lookin' over a fence and he fires at it. An' the next thing we hear is two or three horses gallopin' away, and there's no more shootin'. No one dared go out for quite a while, fearin' some trap. And when we do go out, there we find O'Maley stone dead, shot through the throat.'

Such was the saga of Goimbla, and we actually talked to the man who shot him, and were allowed to have pot shots at wild turkeys with the rifle which shot him. For weeks after we returned home, we gave a lifelike performance of the Drama of Goimbla, Jack and I taking it in turn to play the parts of Mr Campbell and O'Maley, while Flo and Jessie in turn played the part of the heroine Mrs Campbell, running down to the back room to the accompaniment of 'gunshot sound effects' produced by beating a roulade on a kerosene tin.

# Some Adventures

BLACKFELLOWS AND bushrangers must be counted as unusual episodes in life at 'Illalong', but station children lived in Wonderland in those days.

A wild black duck nested under a bush not a hundred yards from the house. Carefully covering up her eggs with a blanket of down from her breast, she went away to feed and, later on, we watched her lead her brood down through the long grass to the creek for their first swim — one of the prettiest sights in Nature. Whether she had told them what to do or whether they acted by instinct is only known to herself, but the little waddling balls of down did not follow her in a group. They spread out in a long single file, the idea evidently being that, if the brood were attacked by any enemy such as a cat or a hawk, only one would be taken; the others would have a chance to plant themselves, and young black ducks are among the most amazing planters in the world. If such a brood were surprised in a small waterhole containing no cover but a few waterlily leaves and a little rough grass growing down to the water's edge, the following things would happen.

The old mother (or if she happened to be a young mother with her first brood, the programme would be just the same); the mother duck would flap out of the water as if crippled and try to lead the children away from her young. The ducklings would disappear as if by magic. At one moment there would be a waterhole full of young ducks; at the next there would not be the sign of a duck, no ripple on the water, no leaf stirring. The dogs could hardly keep from jumping into the water after the young ducks, but, after seeing the parade of the brood down to the water, we would not allow any slaughter of the ducklings.

Bush families in those days, living miles away from a doctor, had hair's-breadth escapes from serious injury; in one school holidays Frank Barton and his friend 'Sid' Blaxland, a nephew of Blaxland the explorer, came up for some duck shooting and, as schoolboys will, they left their powder flasks lying about. This was too good a chance to be resisted and Jack and I commandeered a powder flask containing enough powder to blow our heads off. Luckily we had sense enough not to explode the flask, but we poured the powder out onto a sheet of paper and Jack threw matches at it while I bent over it to see the result. A lightning-like sheet of flame shot up from the powder and I had my eyebrows burnt off, my hair singed, my face blackened and my eyes temporarily closed. Weeping bitterly, I was led home by my cousin — two nice objects to confront a harassed housewife and one can imagine the relief when it was found that my injuries were only superficial.

There was, too, the day when, without meaning the least harm to anybody, we wandered away into the bush and met with the most glorious adventures, ending up with the usual unsatisfactory sequel. First of all, our old half-cattle half-mongrel dog, too slow to catch a bandicoot, 'took after' a kangaroo rat, an animal which could in the ordinary course of events have run clean away from him. To the amazement and delight of his owners, the old dog caught it. An examination of the body showed that it was suffering from a bad injury to one of its hind legs, which accounted for the capture but did not make the dog any less of a hero in the eyes of its owners. Nor was this all; in the very next five minutes old Paddy walked almost on top of another kangaroo rat in its nest, and this one had only just time to jump into a log to save its life. Of course, we had our tomahawks with us, and without taking any account of the flight of time, the distance from home or the thickness of the log, we proceeded to cut it out of its fastness. Two kangaroo rats in one day — what a triumph for Paddy, an animal so little appreciated at home!

We chopped and chopped and chopped until, pausing for a rest, we looked up at the sky and realised that it was almost dark, we were a couple of miles from home and had told no one where we were going. With heavy hearts we shouldered the body of the dead kangaroo rat, which suddenly seemed to weigh as much as a wallaby, and set off on our trudge to the station. Arrived there, the following unpleasant things happened. No one would look at the body of the kangaroo rat or listen to the tale of its capture, nor would anyone accept our explanation that we had not known how late it was while we were chopping at the log. For the first time in our lives we were soundly cuffed and sent to bed after a meal of cold mutton, salted with tears. Hardest of all to bear was the thinly veiled superiority of my sisters, who never seemed to get into any kind of trouble. They had an occupation which kept them out of mischief.

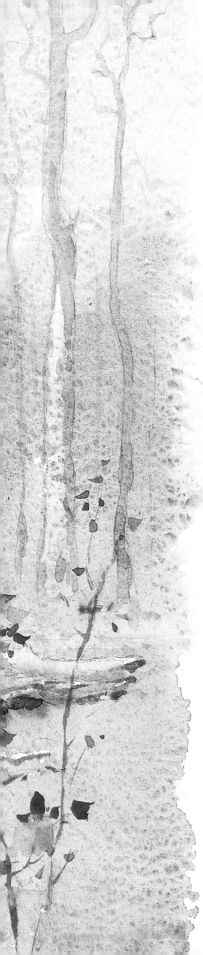

# Storekeeping

PLAYING AT storekeeping has always a charm for children. One gets behind a counter which isn't there and sells tins of imaginary jam, fictitious frocks, and stones for bread to the indulgent buyer. The buyer proceeds to bestow the non-existent goods in a phantom shopping bag and makes a dignified exit.

Playing at shopkeeping is all very well in its way, but how much better was it, as we 'Illalong' children did, to keep a real store and sell meat, flour, tea, sugar and tobacco to real live buyers?

What an aroma hung round the old slab and bark building — an aroma built up of the smell of new boots, harness and saddles of colonial manufacture. There was something all-pervading about the scent of colonial leather in the early days. Then there was the scent of black plug tobacco, so full of nicotine that the plugs stuck together in the hogshead and had to be pried apart with a chisel. The scent of sugar came about third in the list of odours, sugar so slightly removed from molasses that it was full of black sticky lumps, dearly beloved by the blacks. A few blankets, a few rolls of cotton cloth, pickles, jams, tea, sauces, bottles of Farmer's Friend and Painkiller and bags of flour made up the stock in trade — all utilities and no luxuries.

As the heads of the family had but little time to spare, most of the storekeeping was done by the two little girls, Flo and Jessie, then about eight and six years of age; somewhat early to begin storekeeping, one would say, but when a neighbour's boy of fourteen was running a mail contract for the Government, a girl of eight was considered quite competent to sell goods in a store.

Some of the customers were 'travellers', i.e., men seeking work, and they were easily attended to, for the only thing they wanted to buy was tobacco. Meat, flour, sugar, tea, all these things were given free of charge in proportion to the needs of the traveller. In return, the travellers were expected to cut a certain amount of firewood, a request that would not have been made of them at the big 'outside' Queensland stations, but 'Illalong' was an 'inside station', and a little work was expected of every traveller in return for his dole.

Even the smaller of the two little girls could be given the key of the store and could be trusted to sell to a traveller. No choice was needed,

for there was only one brand of tobacco. Quaint characters they were, these travellers, some with Oxford accents and some foreigners barely able to talk English; and the little girls were given jurisdiction to throw in a pair of old boots with a fig of tobacco when they saw the buyer's toes peeping out of his boots. Should a foot be badly chafed, the buyer would be told to go and camp by the creek for a day or two till he was fit to travel, and liberal dabs of ointment would be spread by infant fingers on pieces of linen rag to help the recovery. One might say, as was said of Beatrix Potter's Dormouse, that this was hardly the way to conduct a retail business, but it was the way that the children were encouraged to take, and none of them regretted in after life the lessons they had learnt in dealing with men at the store.

A brief 'thank you' was about all that they ever heard from the travellers, but the station hands were more conversational. For instance, there was John Wilberforce Morley, one of the shepherds, reputed to be an Oxford man who had come down in the world. He never spoke of England, for they had their pride, these children of misfortune, but he must have had some friends in England in good circumstances. Someone sent him, all the way from England, a present of a Russian dog, and if there were many like this dog in Russia, one would feel sorry for the wolves in that country. Shaggy-coated, big-footed, nearly the size of a pony, he had an enormous head with powerful jaws, and he glared out upon the world through a fringe of hair which almost blinded him, but John Wilberforce Morley had an aptitude for dogs. One wonders whether Morley might have disguised his circumstances from his relatives and that they thought they were sending him a most useful present.

Possibly the dog had a certain value in Russia, for, in spite of his Bolshevik appearance, he had an aristocratic name and was registered in the Russian stud books as 'Peter the Great'. Morley was not a conversational character. It was his custom to walk into the store, buy what he wanted and go away again to the dreadful loneliness of his hut on the run without exchanging more than a word or two with the little girls, but the arrival of Peter the Great changed all that. On his first visit to the station after the dog's arrival he began to tell in instalments the saga of Peter the Great. This was the first instalment.

'I'm having a lot of trouble with that dog,' he said. 'He wanted to kill my old sheepdog right straight away. I had to take him out with the sheep on a lead till he got used to my old dog. And then the trouble of feeding him! He eats as much as a horse. Luckily the station sent me out a gun to shoot crows, so I knock over kangaroos and

wallabies and crows and eaglehawks — anything. He even ate a por-cupine after I'd skinned it. Well, it's time I was getting off home. Do you mind telling me what day of the week it is? I've forgotten.'

His next instalment was encouraging. 'Peter the Great is settling down,' he said. 'He hasn't chased anything for a long time, except a kangaroo dog which followed a hawker who came to the hut, and he had no chance in life of catching the kangaroo dog. I'll take half a dozen boxes of matches, please. He brushed all my matches into a bucket of water with his tail.'

Then came the great adventure which set the seal on the fame of Peter the Great. This was before the days of paddocking, and the sheep were shut up in a yard each night. One morning very early, Morley was aroused by a great commotion at the sheep yard, so he

loosed Peter the Great and ran out to find that a big cattle dog from a neighbouring station was in the yard, killing a sheep. Morley's old sheepdog was raising the alarm at the top of his voice, but could do nothing more. This cattle dog fancied himself the equal of any dog that ever stepped, but he had yet to meet a Russian. When he saw Peter the Great, he took to flight and would have got out through a gap in the yard, only that Morley's old sheepdog threw himself on him. Badly bitten, he hung onto the cattle dog long enough to let the slow-moving Peter the Great sink his teeth into the murderer's windpipe, and that was the end of the cattle dog.

Morley had to tell this story to the children every time that he came up to the station, and he told it like an actor, playing the part of each dog in turn, bringing out the alarmed screams of the old sheepdog, the brutal worrying of the cattle dog and the grand finale of the entrance of Peter the Great. Perhaps he had been an actor, for no one ever heard Morley talk of his past: nor did he ever talk of his future until one day he came in and said, very briefly, that he would be leaving the shepherding, as he had been called back to England. He gave no further information, but he said that he would be taking the Russian dog to England with him and would be obliged if the children would look after his old sheepdog for the rest of its life.

From these facts one is able to deduce that Morley was moving into a very much higher sphere than that of a shepherd, and he would have at least one good tale to tell the children in England.

# Wild Life

BEFORE STARTING school, sundry cousins were brought up to help me spend the Christmas holidays and thus it was that we got to know all the birds and animals about the place. Boys and girls, we overran the hilly paddocks, sometimes riding, sometimes on foot.

At the very top of a hill lived an eaglehawk which we children called 'The MacPherson' because he had a hooked beak and a pair of fierce eyes like the picture of a Scottish chieftain in one of our books. Also, like the old-time Scottish chieftains, he had a nasty knack of living upon other people. Mr and Mrs MacPherson never bothered to be civil to anybody and even the crows, who had assurance enough for anything, were afraid to say good day to them lest they might get snubbed. One day one of the blackfellows brought in a young eaglehawk which had fallen out of the nest, and chained it to a perch in the back yard. Here it sat and sulked, scarcely eating anything and letting scraps of its food fall on the ground. Most of the farmyard fowls were afraid to go near it, but Mr Wattles the Muscovy drake, a very pushing sort of person, went in and started to help himself to the scraps on the ground. MacPherson Junior ignored him for a time, but Mr Wattles only breathed heavily and went on eating. The other birds looked on astounded, and Mr Wattles got more and more familiar until at last he pushed right up close to the eaglehawk. Then there was tragedy. A claw like a grappling iron shot out, and the next moment Mr Wattles was dead and the eaglehawk was holding him with one hand and plucking him with the other. He had evidently been brought up properly and he thought that eating Muscovy duck in the feathers was a messy sort of business. Mr Wattles was very unpopular, anyhow.

Further down the hill there were patches of open ground where the spurwing plovers laid their eggs every year, shouting a warning to all and sundry as they wheeled and chattered over anyone who went near their nests. At other than breeding time, the spurwings formed a little clique of their own, very correct in their clothing and demeanour with their black caps and white waistcoats and little yellow protuberances over the beak. My imaginative cousin said that they were a secret society acting under orders, for when one wheeled they all wheeled, and when one talked they all talked. On this open country, too, there lived the curlews, gaunt grey birds with long legs and long necks. Occasionally they wailed like banshees, and she said that they were the souls of lost people asking their way home.

As an offset to the pessimism of the curlews, there was the optimism of the Happy Family, little dark slate-coloured birds like miniature ravens, but the cheeriest people in the bush. They built slovenly nests in the small saplings, all using the same nest, which must have been

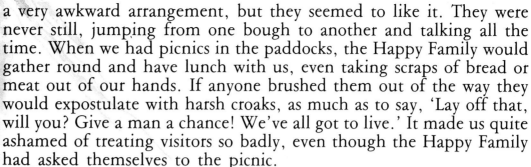

a very awkward arrangement, but they seemed to like it. They were never still, jumping from one bough to another and talking all the time. When we had picnics in the paddocks, the Happy Family would gather round and have lunch with us, even taking scraps of bread or meat out of our hands. If anyone brushed them out of the way they would expostulate with harsh croaks, as much as to say, 'Lay off that, will you? Give a man a chance! We've all got to live.' It made us quite ashamed of treating visitors so badly, even though the Happy Family had asked themselves to the picnic.

Then there were the soldier birds, fierce-eyed little grey ruffians which we called 'policemen birds' as they did their best to keep order in a very disorderly community. Not a crow could sit on a stump but the nearest soldier bird would soon sound the alarm and the others would gather from all over the bush, flying at the crow and striking at him with their little wings until he took himself off. Even The MacPherson himself had no terrors for them and, if he came to rest on a tree in the hope of picking up a young lamb for luncheon, the soldier birds would assail him with cries which sounded like 'thief', 'burglar', 'assassin', like a mob in a Paris riot. Not a snake could leave his lodgings, even though he moved as silently as water flowing over the ground, but the soldier birds were on his trail flying at him and pecking at his head: and no burglar alarm ever brought reinforcements so quickly as the soldier birds' shriek of, 'Snake! Snake!' They were not very pleasant people, the soldier birds, for every one of them was a Nosey Parker, noisy and suspicious, but they made paddocks fairly safe for little feet in the long grass and no human policeman ever did better work. They had earnest, gloomy, fault-finding faces, never happy and never satisfied with themselves, though they risked their lives a dozen times a day.

Magpies were there in plenty, and the same pairs came year after year to build their nests in the trees close to the homestead. One pair in particular grew so tame that they would come and sit on a fence outside the meat-house and would take scraps of meat from the hands of the children. Having made this start, they evidently thought that they might go a little further, and next year they brought their four young children and stood them in a row along the meat-house fence for inspection. Very proud of them they were, too. The young ones thought that this was taking too much of a risk and fluttered away when anyone tried to feed them; but before long, anyone coming out of the house would find the four young ones sitting on the fence uttering the raucous squawk which is the young magpie's way of asking for food.

Seen from below, a magpie's nest looks a clumsy construction of sticks, but if one can look into it, the lining of the nest must involve them in much search. Linings for nests there appeared to be in plenty, what with scraps of wool and the spider threads of the stringybark: but there is evidently some artistic sense about a magpie, some striving after perfection, for when a coir doormat was left outside the house at 'Illalong', the magpies came from far and near, picked it to pieces in a few hours and carried it away to be used as lining for their nests. Those who succeeded in getting pieces of the coir mat must have felt like householders who have acquired a Persian carpet.

Most popular of all birds were the little blue-caps, the males resplendent in blue and black colouring while the females were a sober grey, but sometimes the little grey females discarded their grey dresses and masqueraded in blue and black, to the great annoyance of the children, who thought they had them all sorted out. Their little bottle-shaped grass nests were sacred things, and woe betide the cat who was seen prowling near. Strange to say, these little fellows, the most delicate and dainty of all Australian birds, would come to the very door of the kitchen for tiny scraps of meat.

Then there were the swallows who came back to the house year after year and persisted, in the face of very heavy opposition, in building their mud nests under the verandah. Pieces of cardboard cut into the shape of hawks and hung under the verandah failed to scare them away, and it seemed cruel to keep on destroying their nests. Finally a compromise was reached by nailing pieces of board underneath their nests to catch the droppings, and for years the same pairs of swallows reared their families in comfort and safety.

Besides the people of the woods, there were the people of the water, for the creeks were chains of big waterholes in which the inhabitants splashed and dabbled and swam and dived: wild ducks which spent a lot of their time lazing on the banks; energetic little dabchicks perpetually diving and working hard, though there could not really have been much need for it. Old Man Platypus, very exclusive, as befitted a gentleman of his ancient lineage, went about his business as unobtrusively as possible. Nobody ever heard Mr Platypus make a remark, nor did anyone ever see him make a splash. He swam up the creek against the current without leaving a ripple, or he drifted down it, silently as a brown streak of water-weed. Sometimes, but very rarely, Mr Platypus would come ashore and comb his fur or lie on a patch of warm sand like an old gentleman sunning himself on the verandah of his club. He hated the pushing, noisy rabble, and he was about the only creature in the bush who never attracted the attention of the soldier birds, which meant a lot, for the soldier birds missed very little.

Another friend of the family was 'Oily Gammon' the water rat, so called because he slipped through the water like oil and when anyone was watching him, he would deceive them by diving under water and coming up in some unexpected place under a tuft of grass and weeds. He was quite a dandy with his black satin coat, his white cravat, his buff-coloured face and about three inches of snow-white tip to his tail. He was an aloof sort of person, always hunting alone and never making friends with anybody. The horse boy set himself to catch Oily Gammon in a home-made trap, made by bending down a sapling and fastening it in position with a complicated arrangement of a trigger fixed into a piece of wood. The idea was that when Oily Gammon touched the trigger, it would release the sapling and hoist Mr Gammon up into the air, but Mr Gammon was only caught that way once and then he bit through the cord and released himself. The trap was

set again with pieces of crawfish, but Mr Gammon dug away the soil round the trap and picked the bait out from under the trigger instead of putting his foot on it as he was expected to do. It was most disappointing, except to Mr Gammon, who was spared the trouble of hunting for food.

These were the harmless people of the bush, afterwards to be almost exterminated by poisoned rabbit baits and by foxes. There were bees' nests here too, plenty of them, and an Old Hand, just such another as Jerry the Rhymer, to help us take them. The few that we took made no real difference, for they were all over the place; but when anything gets too prosperous Nature always produces some sort of plague to keep it down, and hives were invaded by a moth which wrought fearful havoc. Sometimes we would fell a tree, to find that the bees had gone and that the ants were gathering the honey.

All these things were by way of education for a youngster and to teach him to look out for trouble when things were brightest. A couple of years at the little bush school were a useful experience: they served as a guide to the thoughts and ideas of the (in those days) inarticulate masses.

# Big Kerrigan

THE FIRST big person I ever met was, naturally, a schoolmaster. To all small boys there is something superhuman about their first schoolmaster, and I was a very small boy, only about eight years old at the time.

The school was situated in a little hamlet called Binalong, where the mail coach used to stop to change horses, and where the gold escort from the Lambing Flat diggings used to create a sensation once a week as it went clattering through the town, with two armed troopers riding in the front and another armed trooper sitting with his carbine across his knees on the box seat alongside the coachman.

It had been a great bushranging district, and the house where Gilbert the bushranger was shot, and the grave of Gilbert in the police paddock, were the two show places of the town. In the warm summer evenings the station hands and house servants would sit out on the wood heap and sing, to the wailings of a concertina, songs about 'Dunn, Gilbert, and Ben Hall', 'The Wild Colonial Boy', and 'Bold Jack Donahoo', and there were any amount of men in the district who would have had a crack at the escort only for the armed guard.

Every morning I had to walk a mile or so up the paddock, freezing with cold in the winter or sweating with heat in the summer, catch my pony, and ride him the four miles into school. Our schoolmaster, Moore by name and Irish to the roots of his teeth, was supposed by us boys to have 'fit in the Fenian rebellion', which was all to the good so far as we were concerned. It was a great Irish district and some of my schoolmates had parents who had been 'sent out' for participating in some similar festivity.

Our schoolmaster and the little wiry Irish police trooper shared the sovereignty of the hamlet between them and they both had a consuming passion for game cocks. Micky Tracey, son of the poundkeeper, said that he had 'sneaked up on them wanst, at the back of the police station so they were, and they fighting game cocks agin each other, and the cocks with steel spurs on'.

We could hardly believe that two men who between them represented law, and literature, and the Government, backed up by the black tracker, would be guilty of such an enormity. But we got an even worse shock later on. One fine day the priest, who drove twenty miles to hold mid-week service, drove his Abbott waggonette and pair of fast ponies into the school yard and went inside, as we supposed, to talk politics and higher mathematics with the teacher. Of course we children swarmed all over his trap and, after pulling out bags of horse feed, surplices, etc., we heard something cackle and, lo and behold, there was a game cock, eyeing us with haughty indifference from his confined quarters in a fruit case!

Well, that priest went into a burning house to save a woman's life, and perhaps the bird was only brought out for comparison and, so to speak, educational purposes. *Honi soit qui mal y pense.*

Then the world, and civilisation, hit us with a bang. The great Southern Railway, connecting Sydney and Melbourne, was built right through the town, and for miles to the north and miles to the south were nothing but torn earth and navvies' camps, and blasts going off, and the clang of temporary rails. Fettlers, gangers, dobbin drivers and construction men all swarmed into our little town, and on a pay Friday not Monte Carlo itself had anything on us when it came to drink and gambling. The navvies didn't consider that they were properly intoxicated till they lost all power of speech or movement, and they used to stagger homewards along the road, bearing bottles, till they fell gloriously in the dust.

I used to train my pony to jump over their prostrate figures on the

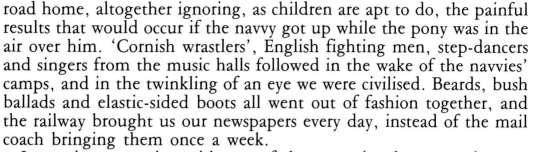

road home, altogether ignoring, as children are apt to do, the painful results that would occur if the navvy got up while the pony was in the air over him. 'Cornish wrastlers', English fighting men, step-dancers and singers from the music halls followed in the wake of the navvies' camps, and in the twinkling of an eye we were civilised. Beards, bush ballads and elastic-sided boots all went out of fashion together, and the railway brought us our newspapers every day, instead of the mail coach bringing them once a week.

It was in connection with one of these navvies, however, that my hero worship received its first shock. There is a slang saying, very common throughout Australia, 'Why go crook of a Monday?' It probably arises from the fact that people are not at their best to face work and worry on Monday after the relaxation of Sunday. Anyway, it was on a Monday that Trooper O'Mara, wearing his uniform, a revolver and a worried expression, came into the little slab schoolroom and started a whispered colloquy with the teacher — or at least they whispered for a while and then, growing excited, they raised their voices. And thus it was that we learnt that 'Big Kerrigan', a celebrated navvy who could lift an anvil and was the champion 'wrastler' of a dozen railway camps, had been drinking steadily through Friday, Saturday, and Sunday and was now at large suffering from delirium tremens.

' 'Tis down by the crick he is,' said the trooper, 'and him wid an axe. He must be locked up or he'll murder somebody or maybe kill himself. I call on you, Mr Moore, in the Queen's name, to assist me to arrest this man.'

Here were our two famous men — O'Mara, who, as we believed, had 'taken' several bushrangers single-handed, and the teacher who had fit in the Fenian rebellion — faced at last with a chance to show their stuff. Bound together as they were by the ties of cock fighting, each must support the other to the death.

To our dismay, the teacher showed every sign of being a conscientious objector. 'I'll not go, O'Mara,' he said. ' 'Tis your job to arrest drunks. 'Tis my job to teach the childerrun. Ye've been carrying that revolver a long time, let us see do ye know how to use it. Ye're an armed trooper of the Queen. Go on and do your job!'

'Yes, and if I shoot him, where'll we be? The railway camps will wreck the town, and when I tell them that I called on ye for assistance and ye wouldn't come, they'll hang the pair of us. Come on! Let ye back up what I say, and if we can coax him into the shed at the back of the court house I could maybe handcuff his arms round the big upright — if so be as he didn't walk away with the whole thing. I've just shifted me turkeys out of it, anyhow.'

For one brief moment, the teacher hesitated. Then, like Caesar jumping the Rubicon, he crossed the room, seized his hat and, taking me by the hand, he set out after the trooper. It has since occurred to me that he took me because I was a magistrate's son and would add a sort of tone to the inquest, if any. Having no orders to the contrary, the other children followed like a small pack of hounds after their master, and thus we set out to arrest Big Kerrigan.

All we knew of his movements was that he had gone down along the creek and he might have left the creek and gone away up into the scrub in the police paddock, or he might have fallen down one of the prospectors' holes that still remained unfilled and unfenced at unexpected and irregular intervals along the flat. But there are always ways of finding things in the bush, and they mostly depend upon birds. A magpie will find you a snake, a crow will find you a dead man and a spurwing plover will locate any other sort of trouble. Sure enough, we heard the plovers shrieking and saw them circling over a clump of big trees at a bend of the creek, and there we found Big Kerrigan.

And even as I saw him, the whole glamour of the adventure dropped away from me. This poor crazed mammoth, with foam on his lips and stark terror in his eyes, dodging in a sort of shuffling run from tree to tree, occasionally swinging his axe to threaten imaginary pursuers, and shouting, 'They're after me, they're after me!' Remember, I was only eight years old, and the horror of the thing made such an impression on me that never since then have I had anything but detestation for those who would sell liquor to a drunken man. But the problem before us was what to do with Kerrigan. A delirium tremens patient of Herculean strength and armed with an axe is a handful for anybody.

Luckily, the trooper was a Master of Arts when it came to dealing with drunks. Slipping his revolver round under his coat 'lest the sight of it might annoy him', he issued his battle orders to the teacher. 'I'll go up an' speak wid him,' he said. 'And if I can get him to come along wid me, do ye close in on his other side, an' we'll just coax him along. I'll not try to put the handcuffs on him. They'd hobble a horse, but they wouldn't go round them wrists of his.'

We children stood breathless as he walked up within five yards of

the giant with the axe. 'Kerrigan! Kerrigan!' he said. Slowly the fear-crazed eyes of the maniac focussed themselves on the trooper, and Kerrigan, trembling like a frightened horse, stood leaning on his axe. 'O'Mara,' he said, the words bubbling out from the foam on his lips, 'ye'll not take me. I can bate ye, I can bate any bastard of a polisman.'

'So ye can,' said O'Mara cheerfully, 'or any two of 'em. But I'm not wantin' to take ye. I've got nothin' agin ye. But ye're not fit to be out here wid no hat and the ants all over ye. Come along wid me, and I'll look after ye.'

For a while, things hung in the balance. A look of suspicion came into his eyes and we expected Kerrigan to spring at the policeman and smash him to pieces with the axe. 'What d'ye want with me?' he said.

'The ganger told me to get ye to come up to my house and give ye a nip of brandy and a wash, and he'll send in for ye. The plate-layin' is all gone to hell, and you away drinkin'. See, now, let one of the childer carry the axe for ye, and I'll walk one side of ye and Mr Moore here will walk the other and we'll keep them off ye. They'll never come near ye, with us here. See, now, give one of the childer the axe to carry and we'll go up and get a nip of brandy.'

And thus was the arrest of Kerrigan effected. Without a word he handed over the axe and, with the trooper on one arm and the teacher on the other, the procession set out for the police station. Now and again Kerrigan relapsed into frenzy and threw his Herculean arms about, sending the trooper and the teacher sprawling in the dust. But the two Irishmen had their blood up and they closed in on him again, hanging onto his arms as killers hang onto the jaws of a whale.

Arrived at the station, a strong nip of brandy reduced the giant to a state of coma, during which his arms were secured round the centre post of the shed by a steel chain. He woke up at intervals during the night, and roared like a volcano, and every time that he did so the dispossessed turkeys on top of the roof gobbled frantically; the fowls woke up and started a cackling chorus like the frogs of Aristophanes; all the dogs in the blacks' camp rushed about barking madly; and Kiley's bull, in his paddock across the road, rumbled his disapproval in a style which indicated that, unless somebody did something pretty soon, he would have to come down and do it himself.

Thus did my teacher justify his claim to be considered my first great man. True, he had at first shrunk back when adventure called, but look how he behaved afterwards!

It was my fate, in later years, to meet many great men — Lord Roberts, Lord French, Lord Kitchener, Rudyard Kipling and Winston Churchill. Would any of them have done any better?

# Home Life

BEFORE GOING any further on this journey, let us consider home life after the railway came; when we were at any rate partially civilised and got mail every day instead of once a week. Speaking of life in the bush, the Australian poet, Brunton Stephens, has told us that 'this eucalyptic cloisterdom is anything but gay', but we managed to enjoy ourselves in our own way.

We outgrew the original homestead of four big rooms and some skillion rooms were added, but, as the family continued to grow, more space was needed, and a four-roomed house was brought in from the holding of a selector who had sold out to the station. This house, not a very large one, was jacked up onto rollers by the bullock driver and a bush carpenter, who were in charge of operations. We watched it coming through the trees swaying like a ship at sea, but holding together. Arrived after its voyage, there was some very delicate work with bullocks, hauling it onto its new foundations. When it is required to move a whole house an inch and a half, a bullock team is hardly the handiest method in the world, but the driver somehow made those bullocks understand what was wanted and when he spoke to them, never raising his voice, they would just put their weight into the yokes an ounce at a time. We children gave all the credit to the two leading bullocks, Rodney and Spot, whom we considered to be as knowing as men and a lot stronger. Slowly, slowly, the building slid into position and the bullock driver's reputation was made.

Compared with the western place, 'Illalong' was poor country, but a previous owner had planted a garden with all sorts of English plants and trees, cypress, holly, hawthorn, and a glorious avenue of acacias. The orchard, too, was a delight, with its figs, walnuts, mulberry trees, cherries, grapes, apples and peaches. In a good season we would fill a clothes basket with grapes or figs, and when the clothes basket was filled there seemed to be just as much fruit as ever.

Sometimes the girls were afraid to gather the figs and grapes because of the bees and hornets which came in thousands to sip the juice from the ripening fruit. The Australian hornet is a man-at-arms, with his red and black banded uniform and his sting like the dagger of a bravo. Not that he would go out of his way to attack anybody, but he was a short-tempered gentleman, and if a small hand gathering fruit happened to touch him he would consider himself insulted and would use his dagger without waiting for apologies. One of the station boys said, 'If it comes to being bit by a snake or stung by a hornet, give me the snake.'

Then there were the birds who insisted on their rights to the fruit: little silver-eyes nibbling away industriously with their tiny beaks; parrots biting slices out of the peaches with their pincer-like jaws; and the leatherheads whose heads and necks were bare of feathers so that they

would not get their plumage in a mess while digging into the fruit. We did not exactly grudge the birds their share but it was disconcerting, while sitting in a fork swaying perilously, to see the silver-eyes and parrots gorging away at the ripest plums and peaches which always grew at the ends of the branches, just out of our reach. The leatherheads were grey birds, bare-necked as vultures and not, apparently, gifted with any brains: and yet they were the most expert nest builders of the lot, weaving long grasses and strips of stringybark into beautiful hanging nests which swung from the twigs right out on the end of the gum tree branches where nobody could climb. Not even the iguana, that terror to small birds, dared trust his weight on the frail twigs where the leatherheads hung their nests, and they built them so high from the ground that Mr Iguana was due for a very nasty fall if the branches gave way with him.

Other fruit lovers were the bower birds, who must have had the collector's instinct, for they built bowers of sticks and lined them with grasses and decorated them with pieces of glass, coloured rags and bright stones. One can imagine the pride with which one bower bird showed to another the neck of a glass bottle, in the days when the necks of glass bottles were none too numerous. However, they did not let their mania for collecting interfere with their appetites and, if they

were a hundred yards away, down at the bottom of the garden, they could scent an apple being peeled in the house and would fly up and sit on the window sill, hoping to get a share of the core or the peelings. They were very friendly people, the bower birds, and were quite prepared to have a fruit lunch with anybody.

But life was not all birds and fruit and flowers. We had to work fairly hard. The girls gathered eggs from the fowls which ran wild all over the place, scores and scores of them, nesting in old barns, under the water tanks, or living the life of Riley as wild birds, never coming near the house and nesting among the masses of variegated thistles in the old sheep yard. Dodging through these thistles after nests, it was nothing unusual to see half a dozen fowls rise up like rocketing pheasants and fly for a hundred yards or so, to the accompaniment of a chorus of cackles from their mates hidden away in the thistle bed. There were no foxes, and, as for the native cats, well, the fowls bred faster than the native cats could eat them. A hundred eggs in a day was just a fair tally, and these eggs had to be put away in lime water as a reserve against the cold weather. Motherless lambs were brought to the house and installed as pets, and when anyone went up the yard he was always beset by lambs wagging their tails and getting in his road. A motherless foal was brought in, shy and frightened at first; but once he felt his feet he took charge of the place, chased the lambs and the dogs, and wound up by chasing the cook out of the kitchen. After this exploit he was judged old enough to go out into the paddocks; and one day a Hindoo hawker came in badly rattled and said that a colt foal had 'sparred up at him like a prize-fighter', and what sort of horses did we keep, anyhow?

The strongest character about the place was the pet white cockatoo known as 'Uncle'. He had been brought in by a black boy who had picked him up when he fell out of the parental nest in the spout of a tree and, as he was only able to flutter a few yards, the boy had caught him and brought him along. 'Plenty savvy, that feller,' said the boy. 'Plenty talk, him know a lot, all same old man.' At first he was most uninteresting, for his only accomplishment was to sit on a perch swaying himself backwards and forwards, keeping up a never-ending complaint 'ah-ah-ah-ah' until we wondered that he did not get a sore throat.

Uncle's life seemed to be just one long complaint until one day we heard our father calling mother from the bottom of the garden. As we knew father was out on the run, it was inexplicable. We ran into the garden thinking that perhaps he had had a fall from his horse and was making his way home; and there we found the cockatoo practising the first words he had learned. His first impersonation was such a success that he soon learned to call the dogs by their names and they, regarding him as a superior intellect, never dared to interfere with him.

Cockatoos spend a lot of their time in digging for yams, and he soon learned to dig up plants or seeds; when washing was put out on the line he would wait till everyone had gone and then he would walk along the clothes line like a man on a tightrope, pulling out the clothes pegs and letting the washing drop on the ground and one day, when he had no other mischief on hand, he was found on the roof patiently loosening, with his powerful beak, the screws which held the sheets of galvanised iron in place. Because he was so full of knowledge, we had called him Uncle Remus, and father said that he was a blessing in disguise for it kept everyone interested to know what he was doing and gave them something to talk about. At any hour of the day someone was liable to say, 'What's Uncle doing?' and it generally turned out that he was in some mischief or other. Sometimes Uncle would go for a fly round the house, but if he went out into the paddocks, the wild cockatoos would have none of him and he had to make the best of his way home, shrieking for help. After these exploits he might be heard whispering softly to himself, like one whose brain has been turned by much meditation. Then he would burst into maniac shrieks of disgust which would be heard a mile away, had there been anyone to hear him.

# Old Edmund

In those days my father managed three properties and was helped by an overseer, Mr Brigstocke, who was the object of my greatest admiration, always riding incredible distances on outlaw horses and taking a fall or two as a matter of routine.

Did word come in that a shepherd had cleared out and left his flock to look after itself, it was always Brigstocke who had to saddle up, sometimes in the middle of the night, and go out and take charge until somebody could be sent to relieve him, and one of the most frequently missing was a celebrity whom we always knew as 'Old Edmund'. He had been convicted of a murder, but had never ceased to protest his innocence, and when any stranger cast up at his hut, Old Edmund always scrutinised him very closely in the idea that the stranger might be the 'Kentish Hero' — the man, who, as Edmund always insisted, had committed the crime. It became an obsession with him and he accused all sorts and conditions of men, including a clergyman.

Finally, he thought he had got the right man, so he left his sheep and tramped twenty miles into Yass to give information to the police. The accused man was an Englishman of the highest respectability and of such an age that if he were indeed the 'Kentish Hero' he must have committed the murder at the age of ten, but this started an investigation into the case and Edmund received a free pardon, a pardon for an offence which he had never committed but it was, apparently, the only way of annulling that conviction. In addition, he was granted a thousand pounds' compensation, the money to be administered by my father as trustee for his benefit.

This started all sorts of trouble, for all Edmund's 'friends' descended on him like crows on a carcass, selling him horses, traps, sideboards (he lived in a mud-floored hut) and enough liquor to wash out the memory of the past. Of course my father had to put his foot down on this, for neither the man's money nor his life would have lasted a month if the boom had been allowed to continue. For a time, my father was so busy with this affair that he had little time to attend to anything else, but gradually things sorted themselves out, and the Australian Dreyfus lived out the rest of his life cleared in character, but never satisfied because he had failed to find the man who did the murder.

The ration cart went out weekly to these shepherds and carried the ten, ten, two, and a quarter (ten pounds of flour, ten pounds of meat, two pounds of sugar, and a quarter of a pound of tea) which we youngsters weighed out for them from the station store, a store full of fascinating things such as greenhide whips, butchers' knives, tobacco, spurs, elastic-sided boots and powerful aperient medicines. The cook at the travellers' hut once got some arsenic to lay baits for native cats, but, being an absent-minded person, he put the packet of arsenic on the shelf above the hut fireplace alongside a packet of baking powder. There were three travellers in the hut that night and, hurriedly mixing them a damper, he put in the arsenic instead of the baking powder, and poisoned the lot of them, including himself. Not that any of them died, for he had put in so much that their stomachs cleared themselves of the poison, but it was a toss-up with them, and Brigstocke — *toujours* Brigstocke — had to ride at full speed twenty miles through the night for the doctor from Yass. It cannot be said that our lives were monotonous or bare of adventure.

Even the household washing did its share in breaking up the monotony. This washing was done by a shepherd's wife about four miles out, and every Monday we packed the spring cart with the washing, our lunches, and a couple of guns, powder flasks, and shot belts in the hope of getting some ducks at the waterhole along the road. One day, while we were packing the cart, a sudden flash of lightning struck a tree alongside the old spring cart horse and started him off up the paddock at top speed. He jumped ten feet down the bank of the creek onto a sand spit, but the cart stood it. Then away he went up the paddock, and following him up we came first on a gun, then on a powder flask, then on somebody's night shirt and other indescribable garments, till we seemed to be following a paper chase, and at the end of it all we came upon the cart jammed between two trees but undamaged, while the old horse in the remains of the harness had caught the reins in a log and was standing there shivering like a leaf.

He could never be trusted to stand unwatched after that, for if anybody dropped as much as a pipe, he was off.

Every morning, cold or hot, wet or fine, I was away before breakfast with my bridle up the horse paddock to catch my pony. Hoar frost like snow lay on the ground in winter, and the dry grass was slippery walking in the summer. Possum tracks led across the grass from one tree to another and one day I found in the spout of a stump a flying mouse, one of the most beautiful of Australian creatures. Parakeets like green and gold projectiles shrieked a greeting as they flashed past, and over all there sailed The MacPherson, the eaglehawk, with his thoughts, like mine, fixed on breakfast. My little fourteen-hand pony was always easy to catch, as he could reckon on getting a handful of hay while his owner was at breakfast. Then off on the four-mile ride to school, up the big hill where Ben Hall the bushranger had stuck up my uncle and everybody who came along, lest they should warn the mail coach of his presence.

There were plenty of people about in those days, and among the travellers that he gathered in was a well-mounted woman who galloped off when his back was turned and defied him to wheel her back. I often wondered whether I would have the nerve to do it if the same thing ever happened to me. Then on past the incurious navvies working on the railway line, past the teamsters and perhaps a mob of travelling sheep with a dog, single-handed, steadying the lead in front.

Behind the mob rode the drovers, sitting loosely in their saddles and sometimes they would stop me and ask, 'What sort of cove was the manager of this place in front; would he dog their sheep through or would he give them a chance to get a feed?'

My pony, which I rode practically every school day for two years, had been bought for two pounds ten, a fair price in those days. He had a remarkable colour scheme of red chestnut blotches on a white ground. So far as anyone knew, he was by an Arab stallion from a Timor pony mare and, like most other old-timers, I hold the opinion that they do not breed such ponies nowadays.

# Uplift at 'Illalong'

WE CHILDREN had any number of chances to study the development of reason or instinct in birds and animals. And, if dogs and birds have their characters, so have sheep. Not that anyone expects much individuality from a sheep, but there came an uplift in the lives of sheep and the 'Illalong' children were privileged to see it.

The merino sheep had been, for centuries, so carefully looked after by shepherds that they had lost the faculty of looking after themselves. They would not even look after their own lambs unless they were shown how to do it.

Thus it came that 'Illalong' in the lambing season had a number of lambing-down camps, each in charge of a careful shepherd. Their business was to shut up the ewes about to lamb in small pens and be on hand 'at midnight hour or Matins prime' to 'mother' the lambs, i.e. to introduce each newly born lamb to its mother and to see that she took to the lamb. Once the ewe allowed the lamb to drink from her and had grasped the idea that she was expected to look after the little creature which she had brought into the world, it was considered safe to allow her and her infant to run out with the rest of the sheep.

We used to enjoy these trips out to the lambing camps. The happenings were so unexpected. It sometimes came about that a newly born lamb would get out of its pen and then it would run away from its mother and would follow after any moving object — a horse and buggy, a man or even a sheepdog. It was amusing to see the harassed look of Glen, the border collie, with a lamb trotting after him. He would cast an appealing look at the visitors as though to say, 'It's not my fault, you know.'

Then came the great revolution in the lives of sheep. Someone suggested that it would be possible to do away with shepherds altogether by turning all the sheep on a station out into big wire-fenced paddocks. Old sheep men looked upon this as one of those newfangled notions which were apt to get people into trouble. 'What about the lambs?' they said. 'Their mothers will leave them and they will all die.'

It was considered unsafe to ride near a mob of ewes and lambs for fear that the lambs would leave their mothers and follow after one's horse, but the new idea promised such a saving in station management that it was decided to try it. I well remember my father's astonishment after his first visit to a paddock wherein lambing ewes were left to their own devices.

'I couldn't have believed it,' he said. 'When I rode up to the first mob, every ewe called to her lamb and the mother and the lamb ran away from me as hard as they could go. They seemed to have changed their natures in a night. And I didn't see a single dead lamb in the paddock.'

And that was how sheep came to run in paddocks instead of needing shepherding. When father was asked if he could explain this sudden change in the intelligence of sheep, he said, 'My only explanation is that when the human race have everything done for them for several generations they lose the capacity for thinking for themselves, and the same thing is true of sheep. The absence of any shepherd has awakened the dormant instinct of the ewes, but I cannot explain why the lambs have suddenly developed such a lot of sense. Perhaps the instinct of self-preservation was dormant in them also.'

Whether or not his explanation was correct, the fact remains that ewes and lambs have continued to breed satisfactorily in paddocks ever since.

# In Drought Time

THE DROUGHT was heavy on the land. Luckily, the hay shed was almost full, and as long as the hay lasted the household stock could be kept alive. Also, there was an oat paddock wherein the oats had sprouted and grown to a height of about three inches before the drought demon came along.

Out in the paddocks, the sheep were living on the edge of starvation by picking up seeds and stalks of plants in which a faint suggestion of moisture still lingered. They nibbled the young shoots of briar bushes and picked up fallen leaves under the kurrajongs. They were so weak that if any sheep, in going through a gate, were knocked down by its companions, it could not get up again. Only in the orchard was there any eatable grass, and not much of that.

We came out after breakfast one morning to find the two brothers Jim and Jack Donnelly, who worked on the station, harnessing up Rose, the old white cart mare.

'Where are you going, Jim and Jack?' we asked.

'We're going to get some weak sheep and put them in the orchard, but yeez can't come along. Old Rose done half a day's work yesterday, bringing in a load of wood, and she told us she didn't want to pull any children. She's too weak.'

When Rose was harnessed, Jim climbed to the seat of the cart, while Jack got on his horse. The two Donnellys were the idols of the children; they were young, unmarried men with the faces of Red Indians and the quick, active step of those who habitually have to get on young horses. The conspicuous thing about their costumes was that they were so inconspicuous: drab-coloured tweed trousers stained with horse sweat; Crimean shirts stained to a dull grey by lifting sheep over fences; 'larstic-side' boots; and shapeless old felt hats kept in place by a twisted cord of horse hair worn under the nose and not under the chin, the nose-strap being for the moment more in favour than the chin-strap.

Such were their externals. Below the surface, they simply reeked with accomplishments. Jim Donnelly could play the mouth organ, while his brother twanged an accompaniment on the Jew's harp. Their choice of these weapons of music was more or less forced on them by the need of having something light and portable in the musical line. Also, they were both good nose-singers (if there is such a word) and it was a delight to the children to sit on the woodheap in the still summer evening while Jim and Jack raised their voices. They did not sing the old bush songs about shearing and droving and camping with lousy Harry on the road to Gundagai. 'Them's only rough things,' they said. 'Listen to this.'

> O, come love come, you need not fear,
> My boat lies on the other shore,
> And all I want is my Sally dear
> And I'll be off to Baltimore.

Neither of them had ever seen a boat, nor did they know whether Baltimore was this side or the other side of the Darling River. The spice of sentiment in the verses must have appealed to their higher natures.

Also they knew all sorts of spirited step-dances taught them by their old Irish father who had been a 'great step-darncer' in his day. Taking position on a solid slab of wood, each brother in turn would make his feet rattle like castanets to the accompaniment of the mouth organ played by his brother. Can it be wondered at that when the youngest girl of the Paterson family was asked by her father 'whom she loved', she said that she loved Jim Donnelly?

But we have left old Rose standing in the harness for a long time while we have described the Donnellys.

As soon as the cart moved off, all the milking herd — cows and calves and half-grown steers and heifers — followed it in a purposeful way. Their wishes were hard to divine, for cows are not credited with much intelligence: in fact, the saying 'a silly cow' is generally regarded as an understatement.

Jack Donnelly explained the mystery. 'They've been trying for days to get into that big paddock where me brother's going! They know that if they wait a while they'll be let in for a pick at the oats, but them oats is all stained with sheep and the cows want to get into the big paddock 'cos they think there's better grass there.'

Sure enough, the whole milking mob, including even the old blind Black Aberdeen cow, was following the cart as though it were full of hay. It might be thought that a blind cow, turned loose in a fairly rough paddock, would not last more than half an hour before falling down the side of a gully or getting herself fast in a barbed wire fence, but nothing of the sort ever happened to her. For years she had come and gone anywhere she wished, sometimes following the mob, but not in the least put out if she happened to lose touch with them. She was a cranky old lady and, if surprised by herself, she would charge towards the sound of the footsteps of any passer-by, always pulling up before she got into any trouble.

Jack Donnelly, as usual, had an explanation. 'Them blind cows has got senses we haven't got,' he said; an unsatisfying explanation, but the only one available.

Alas that the march of the milkers was doomed to frustration. The gate of the big paddock was shut in their faces, and soon we saw Jim Donnelly returning with a spring cart load of weak sheep, which he put in the orchard. The sheep being disposed of, there came the usual cup of morning tea for the brothers and, while this was being assimilated, one of the little girls said, 'Jim Donnelly, do you love sheep?'

'Oh, yes, I love 'em, all right,' he said, 'but I wouldn't die of a broken heart if I never saw another sheep. I've managed to do without 'em. Cattle now, them's different. Cattle have sense. You seen them old milkers, they had it all thought out about getting into that paddock. You never seen a sheep with two eyes as clever as that old blind cow that can't see at all. Me old father was out in Queensland when he was a boy and he told us about cattle. He says that, if the wind is blowin' right, cattle can smell water twenty miles away and once they've been to a place they never forget the track. He says that ''Illalong'' wouldn't make a horse paddock for a Queensland cattle station, and the cattle mobs think nothin' of goin' out twenty miles to any part of the run they've ever been before.

'Well, me father was only a boy and didn't know the run, and nobody in Queensland never tells a boy nothin'; it makes 'em smarter if they're left to find things out for themselves. And there was a jackaroo there had to take a mob of cattle up to a place they called the Chain of Ponds, ten miles away, and he'd been there before so of course they reckoned he could find his way again. So, there's me father and a black boy and this jackaroo, all dressed up with breeches and boots and a silk 'andkerchief round his neck like the pictures of jackaroos in books. I never seen a live jackaroo like that, and neither did my father till he seen this one.

'Well, off they go, with the jackaroo riding behind the mob and the black boy smoking some niggerhead tobacco and me father a bit sick with smoking it too: and the black boy didn't know where they were going, and even if he had known he wouldn't have been game to tell the jackaroo anything.

'So, after a while, the cattle begin to grumble down in their throats, like cattle does, and now and agen they'd let a bellow out of them. And me father knows there's somethin' the cattle don't like, but he don't know what's on their minds. Well, there they were, making for the Chain of Ponds across open bush, one mile of it just like the last: and after a while, me father can tell by the sun that the cattle is changing their direction, swinging round little by little till at last they are making back for the place they had started from, but the jackaroo doesn't notice it and one direction is just as good as another to the black boy. And the cattle stops grumblin' and they're hitting out somethin' surprisin', when they oughta be gettin' slower and slower: and then me father sees the station manager coming full split through the bush on a horse. He gallops up to the jackaroo, and me father says this station manager was a very vilent man.

' "Dr Livingstone, I presoom", he says to the jackaroo, grindin' his teeth. "You silk-'andkerchiefed imitation of a crockery doll, what made you bring the cattle back? Don't you know you're within half a mile of the head station? I suppose you reckoned there wasn't any restyrongs out at the Chain of Ponds, so you came back home. Is that it?"

'Well, they go home, and that night a blackfellow comes in from the Chain of Ponds and he says the water is all dried up there, and that was what made the cattle turn back. They couldn't smell any water. An' the jackaroo reckoned he'd saved the cattle a twenty-mile trip for nothin', but I reckon it was the cattle saved the jackaroo. You can have all the sheep you want, Miss Flo, give me cattle.'

# Pet Lambs

THE SEASON was very dry; clouds used to come up and move in a stately procession round the horizon, but the best they could do was to produce a 'Darling shower', i.e., a heavy wind and a dust storm. A rainless winter was followed by a rainless spring, and, lo, it was shearing time. With no railway within a hundred miles of the place, it was not possible to bring in food from the coast and no grass could be rented because all the district wanted whatever grass they had for their own sheep.

The ewes were the problem. A station may lose many sheep in a drought, but so long as the ewes can be saved, there is always a chance of breeding up a new lot of sheep. There are a lot of risks about shearing ewes in lamb, but the risks had to be faced.

That was the reason why Jack Donnelly, boundary rider in charge of the ewe paddocks, brought in the first lot of ewes to be shorn, in great heat, with his dogs limping behind him, lamed by the thorns and spiny burrs which seem to flourish just as well in a dry season as in a good one.

On his way to the shearing shed, Jack gave the mob a rest while he chatted with us.

'It's not going to be too good,' he said. 'These are maiden ewes, and a maiden ewe never worries much about her lamb. If she is strong, and the lamb is strong, they will do all right; but if the ewe is weak and the lamb is too weak to follow her, they git separated and the lamb is lost. Come on, dorgs, coax 'em along slow and give 'em a chance.'

The next morning he reported that twenty lambs had been born during the shearing, and that fifteen of them had been unclaimed by their mothers. A small patch of stunted oats had been kept for emergencies and the ewes and lambs were put in on the oats to give the ewes a chance to pick up their lambs. It was a vain hope. The ewes ate ravenously of the oats, but night fell with the fifteen lambs still unclaimed. It was here that we took a hand. Why shouldn't we rear the lambs on the bottle? True, the cows were not giving much milk, but we were quite ready to go without milk so as to give the lambs a chance. And were there not several tins of condensed milk in the

store? One tin of condensed milk, mixed with a proper proportion of warm water, would feed a lot of lambs. Why not let us try it?

We pleaded so earnestly that father had not the heart to refuse us. 'Very well,' he said, 'you can try it. It will do you no harm to learn a little about lambs.'

We were wild with delight. 'You drive the lambs up here, Jack,' we said. 'We'll make a yard for them on the corner of the garden fence with that spare piece of wire netting.'

'Drive the lambs up here, is it?' said Jack. 'I'd want three racehorses to drive them lambs up here. They'll run like greyhounds in all directions for about a hundred yards and then they'll lay down. I'll bring them up here in the cart, that's the only way anybody could drive them. And do yeez be gettin' your yard ready, and ye'll want to mix a little castor oil with their milk, 'cos lambs that have never drunk from their mothers will never do no good without they get castor oil.'

It was just falling dark when old Rose, the white cart mare, appeared at the gate with a load of fifteen squalling lambs. People wonder how a ewe can distinguish her lamb's call out of a thousand. If they could have heard the variety of tone and pitch used by those fifteen lambs, they would wonder no longer.

The yard was ready, a yard made of wire netting with chaff bags tied to the netting on the windward side, in case of a cold wind coming up in the evening. The lambs were lifted out of the cart and dropped in the yard, and thus began the great lamb rearing experiment.

An unattractive mixture of milk, warm water and castor oil was first prepared and was put into feeding bottles, just the same sort of feeding bottles as are used for babies. Then we realised that it was all very well to take milk to a lamb, but quite another thing to make it drink. Jack and I each had a feeding bottle in one hand and a lamb held between the knees ready for its drink, but would the lambs drink? Of all squirmers and contortionists in this world, there are no better squirmers and no better contortionists than young lambs. As a lamb's mouth was held open with one hand and the feeding bottle presented with the other, the lamb would duck its head, drop on its knees, or wriggle out from between our knees.

Said Flo, 'You're spilling it all. There's milk, castor oil and water all over the ground and all over your clothes. And I don't think the lambs have got a drop of it.'

'Very well,' said Jack, 'you have a go at it.'

'Me have a go at it, and me in this frock? You ought to have more sense.'

'Have it your own way,' said Jack, 'but we mustn't let them beat us. One of you girls hold this lamb while I give it a drink.'

Nor was this much better. The lamb swallowed about a tablespoonful and seemed to be enjoying it, judging by the ecstatic wigglings of its tail. Then it choked and wriggled out of Flo's hands, giving her dress a liberal spray of the mixture.

The situation was tense. We had expected a nice pastoral scene — and now this! We worked on in grim silence, and as each lamb was induced to swallow its allowance of milk it was dropped into the lower half of a galvanised iron tank to prevent its being mixed up with the unfed lot. What a prospect! To the wails of the lambs waiting outside, there was added the clatter of the hoofs of those inside the tank, the tense faces of the children each holding a struggling lamb, and the whole scene lighted up by a smoky hurricane lamp. We saw a vista of days stretching before us in which this programme had to be gone through three times a day!

But the old song says, 'Hope comes with the morning, rest with the night'; when we walked up at sunrise next morning to the loose-box where the lambs had spent the night, we were greeted with a chorus of appealing voices, voices which seemed to convey some hint of gratitude. Could it be true? Could the lambs have appreciated what had been done for them? They say that the elephant never forgets, and the same is true of any young animal which has once been fed. As soon as the loose-box was opened, there came a wave of lambs, all bleating frantically and all trying to get at the bottles. As each lamb was seized and the bottle presented to its lips, the india-rubber pipe conveying the milk was seized by three or four eager mouths. We had our fingers sucked, mumbled or bitten, for lambs are born with teeth (very small ones, it is true, but still teeth). Lambs jostled and pushed each other in a domineering style, in great contrast with their helpless appearance. The whole operation of feeding was over in half the time taken on the previous day and only a quarter as much milk was spilt. Full and satisfied, the lambs lay down in silence to sleep and we were able to get in half an hour's housework before going in to breakfast.

One can imagine what a relief it was to find that the lambs were taking to their feed, but our troubles were not yet over. By dint of putting their drink out in shallow troughs, the feeding bottles were done away with, but the lambs did not thrive. They grew thinner and thinner and bleated more and more feebly. It looked as though, after all our work, we were going to lose the lot. We could have cried.

Just as things were at their blackest, Jim Donnelly paid us a visit. He watched the lambs drinking from their troughs, and then he said, 'Pollard. That's what they want. Give 'em pollard. My old mother's a great one for rearin' lambs. Many a score she's saved and she always puts a little pollard in with their milk. Let ye try the pollard.'

So the pollard was tried, and the change was marvellous. Instead of a lot of spindling hopeless little creatures, the lambs became a fine healthy lot, so vigorous, so noisy, and so much inclined to get into everybody's road that they had to be banished to the stable to keep them out of the way. We were so proud of having reared the lambs that we made no protest about their banishment, nor did we raise any objections at having to go up to the stable to feed them.

We had done something in earnest, for the lambs were worth a pound a head in the market after the drought, and we felt a warm glow of satisfaction when, as they were passing in a mob of sheep, several of the rescued lambs ran out of the mob and tried to suck our fingers.

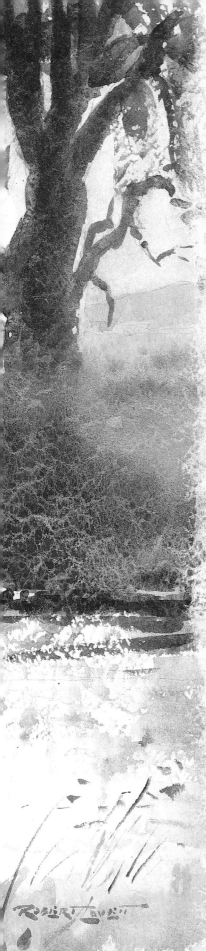

# Of Dogs and Crawfishing

MY FIRST introduction to the dog world was when, as a small boy, I used to go out into the paddocks with an old time-expired labourer who did odd jobs about the station, accompanied always by his two dogs. Horses he feared and detested, but his dogs were the fear of his foes and the admiration of his friends. These dogs were like himself, very English and very rough and hairy. He called them 'Smiffield collies' but they were really English Rough sheepdogs — and rough is about the right word. They had no tails, and if they caught any wild animal they would tear it in pieces. This massive old man was unable to read and write, had never been in a train, and never spoke of his past, which had been hectic enough, with wild nights on the diggings and with fights in the navvies' camps. His two dogs were much like himself, strong and silent, making friends with nobody. They were a quaint trio, but they fitted in somehow with the background of the bush with its eerie silences and its occasional kindliness.

Then we got a dog of our own, a dog with Scottish sheepdog blood in his veins, but he was what the Indians call 'a failed B.A.' in the sheep line, being too rough with sheep even for the easygoing ideas of those days. After his late owner had given him a hiding for biting sheep, he attached himself to us and, as often happens with children's dogs, he developed unexpected abilities. He became something of a retriever, going into the water after sticks; something of a coon dog, going out with us in the moonlight after possums; and something of a pointer, for when we could persuade anyone to go out with us with a gun he would make quite a creditable point at a kangaroo rat lying in its nest. If there were no gun, he would rush straight in on the kangaroo rat, hoping to grab it before it got under way.

Apart from the paddocks, the river held great attractions for us, and one of our favourite sports was catching crawfish.

Our expeditions were very simply fitted out. Four feet of twine and a piece of raw meat made a line for each child. The dogs, by nature very inquisitive, were wild with excitement to know what it was all about. Shooting they knew, mustering they knew and kangaroo hunting they knew, but this was something new altogether.

I recall one such expedition very clearly. The old pony mare, on which all the family had learned to ride, was pressed into the service of carrying the picnic baskets on a pack saddle, but she had her own ideas of what was due to her dignity and importance and, just to assert herself, she got to work and threw the pack, snorting with indignation. We pacified her with endearments and compliments, and the pack was restored after a broken bottle of milk had been replaced. Our expedition started, encouraged by the assurance from old King Billy that 'plenty that feller yabby sit down longa big waterhole'.

Arrived at the waterhole, positions were selected under the shade of big willow trees, the lines were thrown in, and all was expectation and excitement. After a while, one line began to move out very slowly, which meant that old Mr Crawfish had taken hold and was trying to drag away the bait to his hole. Slowly and with a very delicate touch, the line was drawn in and the whiskers and goggling eyes of old Mr Crawfish appeared on the surface.

The true art of crawfishing consists of putting the hand behind the crawfish and scooping him out onto the bank. This can be done just as effectively and more safely by using a net or tin dipper, but this would have spoiled the fun. Even when they were on the bank, coolness and judgment were required to pick them up just behind the wildly waving claws and to drop them into the bucket. They saw it right out to the bitter finish, too, and on this occasion we left the bucket on a slope and, before anyone knew anything about it, the crawfish had struggled out onto the grass and were all making for the water at an indignant crawl. In the excitement our dog sat down on a crawfish so occupied and in a moment he was off for home, yelling loudly with the crawfish hanging onto him.

Sometimes we engaged in another form of this sport, wading in a shallow rocky pool and turning over the stones and pinning the quarry to the ground with a forked stick. This required a nice eye and considerable judgment of distance under water. Thus passed the day, wading and turning over stones while the crawfish made unexpected backward starts with unerring aim to the shelter of another stone.

A wholesale and unsporting way of catching them was to lower a shin of beef in a bag to the bottom of the creek and come along some hours later and haul it out while the Company of Associated Crawfish were still engaged on their dinner, but we never felt comfortable if we employed this method — we liked Mr Crawfish to give us a run for our money.

# The Rescue

FOR TWO years in succession, Mr and Mrs Tom-tit had built a nest in the pepper tree within ten feet of the homestead. It was safer there than out in the bush where native cats, crows, and sparrowhawks made the lives of small birds very precarious. And then a third year arrived and they returned to the old pepper tree, which had served them so well in the past.

To the human eye, there did not seem much wrong with either of the two old nests. True, the wind and weather had knocked them out of shape; the linings where the previous families had been reared were very worn and likely to let the wind through on the eggs; but the framework, if such a term could be applied to a structure of grass, was quite intact. Could it be repaired for this year's nest?

And it is just here where small birds differ from human beings. Humans resort to all sorts of devices to avoid trouble; little birds find pleasure in the work of building a nest, so a new nest it had to be and the pair started to twist their grass stems and invaluable bits of thread, so easy to handle, as mooring ropes round the twigs of the pepper tree.

The small architects must have felt annoyed when a dry stick fell from one of the upper branches of the tree right onto their nest, but this proved a windfall in every sense, for the ends of the stick were securely caught in the branches. They at once moored their nest to it, thus getting a foundation for the top of their nest, while a twig about an eighth of an inch in diameter gave support at the lower end. There was much twittering until this decision was arrived at, but once the point was settled the building went on with great speed. These particular tom-tits always build a nest with a lower and upper compartment. In the lower the hen hatches her eggs and rears her young, while the upper compartment is, in the opinion of the bush people, built with the idea of deceiving the cuckoos, who have a pernicious habit of laying an egg in other birds' nests. A cuckoo's egg laid in the upper compartment would do nobody any harm.

By and by came hatching time, and then the troubles of the tom-tits were trebled. From dawn till dark they toiled, bringing infinitely small mouthfuls of microscopical food to their family. Then came the day when the family, fully fledged duplicates of their parents, were ready to go on their first solo flight. They had strengthened their wings by short experimental flights from one twig to another.

Now came the great adventure.

Do parent birds talk, and do child birds listen? The parents made plenty of noise, chirping excitedly, but the babies appeared as dazed as young aeroplanists going up for the first time. At last one took his courage in hand and followed his mother to the nearest tree, crossing a small pond en route. It was a short enough flight, but when one is very small indeed a flight across a small pond takes on the appearance of crossing the Atlantic.

Two others made the trip safely, but there is always a backward child in every family, and the last of the brood put no style into his work. He fluttered desperately and might have got across only that a puff of wind checked him just when he was most tired and, like a piece of windblown thistle leaf, he fell right into the centre of the pond.

It was a frightful situation. The parents sounded their alarm notes (quite different from their ordinary twitter), but what chance was there of making themselves understood?

It so happened that there was a chance. Flo and Jessie were playing in the garden with old Nan, the Irish setter, an unappreciated artist if ever there was one. Father was too busy to look after her education and we children had no knowledge of a setter's gifts. Nan, quite untrained, would 'set' to a quail in the garden and we would say, 'Go on, Nan, what are you stopping for?'

After a time Nan gave us up as hopeless and took to following anybody who left the station on a horse. One would expect a setter to be a restful sort of animal, but Nan was a sort of canine steam engine, ranging wide of the horse for hour after hour, covering incredible distances in a day. Every now and again she would scent game, a kangaroo rat sleeping in his little grass nest or a curlew standing immobile, hoping to be unnoticed. These Nan would set for a few seconds, always hoping for a word of command. Getting no orders, she would resume her headlong sorties.

Canine artists such as gun dogs and sheepdogs are born with the urge to work, to exhibit whatever talent Nature has given them. Failing anyone to take an interest in him, a young sheepdog will herd fowls from one enclosure to another, and a young gun dog will 'set' or 'point' whatever sort of game comes before him. Poor old Nan! She would lie before the fire in the winter evenings, whimpering in her dreams over her wasted gifts.

Young as the girls were, they had learned to distinguish the notes of birds, so they set off, followed by Nan, to see what was happening. They soon saw that a very small bird was drowning before their eyes, and the pool was forbidden water to the children, but children in the bush learn to think things out for themselves.

The problem was to get Nan to go in for the little bird, and suddenly Flo had a brainwave. She stooped down and picked up a stone and threw it into the pool alongside the struggling infant. Nan saw the splash and bounded in like a Newfoundland dog going to rescue a drowning boy.

When Nan reached the place where she had seen the splash, the stone had disappeared and nothing was left on the pool but the baby tom-tit, almost too small to be worth retrieving; but rather than make a fruitless voyage, she thought she might as well bring home the bird. Fortunately, her instinct had taught her to take the greatest care of everything that she retrieved — she would even carry an egg in her mouth without breaking it — and the little bird disappeared in one gulp of the great red slobbery mouth and she headed for the shore. The parents raised a more agonised squawk than ever when they saw their child gulped down by a marine monster, but they need not have

worried. The bird was as safe in Nan's mouth as if it were in the nest. Three strokes of her great limbs and she walked up the bank of the pool and dropped a bedraggled but uninjured bird at the feet of the children. This stirred the parent birds to a last outburst of clamour; after seeing their offspring delivered from a marine monster, it was now to meet a dreadful death at the hands of a land monster.

Carefully, Flo dried it with her handkerchief and put it on a stump well away from the water. The old birds flew down and fussed over it till it was strong enough to flutter up to the nest, and the episode was ended. The only sad thing about the whole affair was that the old setter, Nan, never knew that she had saved a life.

# The Parrot's Nest

THE LITTLE green and gold parakeets flashed like jewels through the sunshine, going so fast that it took two men to watch them, one to say, 'Here they come,' and the other to say, 'There they go'; but, like all other birds at that time of year, their minds were on rearing a family. They were such carefree little fellows that it was hard to regard them as being serious about anything.

All the time that they were going at such headlong speed, and even when they were hanging to the ends of the gum tree branches sucking honey from the blossoms, their eyes were on the various dead spouts which are common to all gum trees. To make a nest they had to climb into one of these spouts and clear away the old rotten wood and dust which had once been solid timber. This they would excavate with their beaks until they could go down the spout for a foot or so, where their young would be fairly safe. On this unpromising foundation of dust and rotten wood they would lay their white eggs, for the egg of a highly coloured bird is nearly always white.

The parakeets lacked ambition. They lived on honey until the ringbarking of the gum trees made honey scarce, then they took to eating fruit, making many enemies for themselves thereby.

Most parakeets breed well away from houses, but it so happened that one pair of parakeets with, perhaps, less sense than the others, selected a spout in a dead tree close to 'Illalong' homestead for their nest. We say that perhaps they had less sense than the others but, as things turned out, they might have had more. We watched their proceedings with interest and all went well until one day Jack saw a strange sight. He saw a crow, one of the most detested birds in the bush, hanging by its claws to the spout which contained the young parakeets and tapping like a woodpecker at the entrance. The crow's object was a mystery. The spout was only large enough to admit a parakeet, and the crow had no chance of getting down it to seize the young fledgelings. What, then, was the crow's idea in wasting his time tapping on the doorway of a parakeet's nest? Crows have more brains than most other birds, and they do not waste their time in tapping on dead timber.

In his own line of business, which consists solely of getting his living, the crow has no superior in the bird world; at all-round sagacity a white cockatoo would beat him easily, however. Jack stood and watched the crow tapping for a while. Nothing happened and the crow flew away without any remark, leaving a very much puzzled little boy behind him. Returning to the house, Jack found that Mr Masson, the Government surveyor, had arrived on his annual visit. Mr Masson was a good run-of-the-mob surveyor, but his special talent lay in his knowledge of birds and animals. Anything that walked, flew, climbed, dived, or burrowed was an open book to Mr Masson. Also, there were few to equal him with a shotgun. There were no motor cars in those days, and he did all his travelling in a four-horse waggonette driven by one of his staff. Should a quail rise out of the long grass by the roadside, Mr Masson could pick up his gun and bring down the quail while the waggonette was still being driven at full trot; and if anybody thinks that an easy feat, well, he is welcome to his opinion.

To him Jack confided his problem about the crow, and Mr Masson, who had been a small boy himself and was still a small boy at heart, listened with great interest. 'Tapping at the door of a parrot's nest, was he? He knew that the young parrots, if they were old enough, would come to the door of the nest to get fed; and there they would find Mr Crow, and instead of being fed they would be eaten. This is an old trick of Mr Crow. I suppose the young parrots must have been asleep, so Mr Crow flew away. He will go back there tomorrow and we will see what can be done about him. I know a trick that might surprise even Mr Crow.'

The next day two waggonettes started out from the station for a bush picnic. In one waggonette were Mr Masson and his staff; the other was filled with the family from the station. We had very faint hopes that anyone would be able to outwit a crow, and father said in joke, 'If you shoot that crow, Mr Masson, I'll eat it!'

'If I shoot that crow,' said Mr Masson, 'I'm afraid I cannot let you eat it. I want to nail his body up on the trees so as to scare away other crows.'

When we arrived at the tree where the parakeets had made their nest the provisions were unpacked and Mr Masson's cook made a fire to boil the billy. 'Now', said Mr Masson, 'you see that fire? As soon as the smoke goes up, every crow within miles will see it and will come overhead. And even those crows which are too far away to see it will see the others coming this way and will follow them. Tell one crow anything and you tell them all. They have as good a signal system as any army. But I do not expect to bring any great crowd of crows today, for at this time of year each pair keeps to its own patch of country unless they smell a dead bullock or something that makes it worth their while to fly a long way. We may only see a few crows, but they will be the ones we want.'

The picnic was over, the gear was packed in the waggonettes and all the party climbed into their seats except Mr Masson. He drew his gun and cartridges from the tail of his waggonette and put fresh sticks on the fire.

'You all drive away,' he said. 'I am going to plant myself under that bush. Crows cannot count above five, so when they see the waggon-ettes go away they will think we have all gone. They will come up from one tree to another and, when they see no one about, they will fly down to see if there are any scraps left. They are so used to getting scraps from luncheon parties that they almost think they have been invited. They will get a shotgun lunch if they come down today.'

So this was the trick which was to be played on Mr Crow. He was to be brought into range in the belief that there was nobody left about the camp.

We all drove out of sight of the camp, but we could still see the treetops about it. Suddenly there was a thrill of excitement when a crow dropped down from the blue sky and sat on the top of a dead tree. By and by another crow dropped down from the sky and he, too, sat on a nearby tree, and there they remained, watching and waiting. Not a sound could be heard, not a movement seen at the camp.

Then other crows could be seen, wheeling about, and the first two crows decided to come down without any delay. If they waited there would be a crowd of crows at a banquet, barely enough for two.

We watched them fly down and throw themselves backwards in the air at the sight of something they saw on the ground; then there were two shots and the two crows were almost blown to pieces in the air.

So died two detestable villains, who had taken just one chance too many; and the parakeets were free to fly headlong through the trees and gather food for their young in the almost certain hope of finding them alive on their return.

All good things must come to an end, however, and shortly after this adventure I was sent to school in Sydney, where I lived, during term-time, with my grandmother at Gladesville. Here I spent many happy days on the Parramatta River and at the Old Sydney Cricket Ground, but, as Mr Kipling says, that is another story.